W9-ATK-741

# Google® Top 100

# Simplified®

## TIPS & TRICKS

by Joe Kraynak

Visual

WILEY

Wiley Publishing, Inc.

# Google®: Top 100 Simplified® Tips & Tricks

Published by
Wiley Publishing, Inc.
111 River Street
Hoboken, NJ 07030-5774

Published simultaneously in Canada

Copyright © 2005 by Wiley Publishing, Inc., Indianapolis, Indiana

Library of Congress Control Number: 2004112346

ISBN: 0-7645-7697-6

Manufactured in the United States of America

10 9 8 7 6 5 4 3 2 1

1K/RW/RR/QU/IN

No part of this publication may be reproduced, stored in a retrieval system or transmitted in any form or by any means, electronic, mechanical, photocopying, recording, scanning or otherwise, except as permitted under Sections 107 or 108 of the 1976 United States Copyright Act, without either the prior written permission of the Publisher, or authorization through payment of the appropriate per-copy fee to the Copyright Clearance Center, 222 Rosewood Drive, Danvers, MA 01923, 978-750-8400, fax 978-646-8600. Requests to the Publisher for permission should be addressed to the Legal Department, Wiley Publishing, Inc., 10475 Crosspoint Blvd., Indianapolis, IN 46256, 317-572-3447, fax 317-572-4355, E-mail: brandreview@wiley.com.

## Trademark Acknowledgments

Wiley, the Wiley Publishing logo, Visual, the Visual logo, Simplified, Read Less - Learn More, and related trade dress are trademarks or registered trademarks of John Wiley & Sons, Inc. and/or its affiliates in the United States and other countries. Google is a trademark of Google, Inc. All rights reserved. Openwave and the Openwave logo are trademarks or registered trademarks of Openwave Systems, Inc., used by permission. All other trademarks are the property of their respective owners. Wiley Publishing, Inc. is not associated with any product or vendor mentioned in this book.

## Contact Us

For general information on our other products and services, please contact our Customer Care Department within the U.S. at 800-762-2974, outside the U.S. at 317-572-3993 or fax 317-572-4002.

For technical support, please visit www.wiley.com/techsupport.

LIMIT OF LIABILITY/DISCLAIMER OF WARRANTY: THE PUBLISHER AND THE AUTHOR MAKE NO REPRESENTATIONS OR WARRANTIES WITH RESPECT TO THE ACCURACY OR COMPLETENESS OF THE CONTENTS OF THIS WORK AND SPECIFICALLY DISCLAIM ALL WARRANTIES, INCLUDING WITHOUT LIMITATION WARRANTIES OF FITNESS FOR A PARTICULAR PURPOSE. NO WARRANTY MAY BE CREATED OR EXTENDED BY SALES OR PROMOTIONAL MATERIALS. THE ADVICE AND STRATEGIES CONTAINED HEREIN MAY NOT BE SUITABLE FOR EVERY SITUATION. THIS WORK IS SOLD WITH THE UNDERSTANDING THAT THE PUBLISHER IS NOT ENGAGED IN RENDERING LEGAL, ACCOUNTING, OR OTHER PROFESSIONAL SERVICES. IF PROFESSIONAL ASSISTANCE IS REQUIRED, THE SERVICES OF A COMPETENT PROFESSIONAL PERSON SHOULD BE SOUGHT. NEITHER THE PUBLISHER NOR THE AUTHOR SHALL BE LIABLE FOR DAMAGES ARISING HEREFROM. THE FACT THAT AN ORGANIZATION OR WEBSITE IS REFERRED TO IN THIS WORK AS A CITATION AND/OR A POTENTIAL SOURCE OF FURTHER INFORMATION DOES NOT MEAN THAT THE AUTHOR OR THE PUBLISHER ENDORSES THE INFORMATION THE ORGANIZATION OR WEBSITE MAY PROVIDE OR RECOMMENDATIONS IT MAY MAKE. FURTHER, READERS SHOULD BE AWARE THAT INTERNET WEBSITES LISTED IN THIS WORK MAY HAVE CHANGED OR DISAPPEARED BETWEEN WHEN THIS WORK WAS WRITTEN AND WHEN IT IS READ.

FOR PURPOSES OF ILLUSTRATING THE CONCEPTS AND TECHNIQUES DESCRIBED IN THIS BOOK, THE AUTHOR HAS CREATED VARIOUS NAMES, COMPANY NAMES, MAILING, E-MAIL AND INTERNET ADDRESSES, PHONE AND FAX NUMBERS AND SIMILAR INFORMATION, ALL OF WHICH ARE FICTITIOUS. ANY RESEMBLANCE OF THESE FICTITIOUS NAMES, ADDRESSES, PHONE AND FAX NUMBERS AND SIMILAR INFORMATION TO ANY ACTUAL PERSON, COMPANY AND/OR ORGANIZATION IS UNINTENTIONAL AND PURELY COINCIDENTAL.

WILEY

Wiley Publishing, Inc.

**U.S. Sales**

Contact Wiley at
(800) 762-2974 or
fax (317) 572-4002.

# PRAISE FOR VISUAL BOOKS

"I have to praise you and your company on the fine products you turn out. I have twelve Visual books in my house. They were instrumental in helping me pass a difficult computer course. Thank you for creating books that are easy to follow. Keep turning out those quality books."
*Gordon Justin (Brielle, NJ)*

"What fantastic teaching books you have produced! Congratulations to you and your staff. You deserve the Nobel prize in Education. Thanks for helping me understand computers."
*Bruno Tonon (Melbourne, Australia)*

"A Picture Is Worth A Thousand Words! If your learning method is by observing or hands-on training, this is the book for you!"
*Lorri Pegan-Durastante (Wickliffe, OH)*

"Over time, I have bought a number of your 'Read Less - Learn More' books. For me, they are THE way to learn anything easily. I learn easiest using your method of teaching."
*José A. Mazón (Cuba, NY)*

"You've got a fan for life!! Thanks so much!!"
*Kevin P. Quinn (Oakland, CA)*

"I have several books from the Visual series and have always found them to be valuable resources."
*Stephen P. Miller (Ballston Spa, NY)*

"I have several of your Visual books and they are the best I have ever used."
*Stanley Clark (Crawfordville, FL)*

"Like a lot of other people, I understand things best when I see them visually. Your books really make learning easy and life more fun."
*John T. Frey (Cadillac, MI)*

"I have quite a few of your Visual books and have been very pleased with all of them. I love the way the lessons are presented!"
*Mary Jane Newman (Yorba Linda, CA)*

"Thank you, thank you, thank you...for making it so easy for me to break into this high-tech world."
*Gay O'Donnell (Calgary, Alberta, Canada)*

"I write to extend my thanks and appreciation for your books. They are clear, easy to follow, and straight to the point. Keep up the good work! I bought several of your books and they are just right! No regrets! I will always buy your books because they are the best."
*Seward Kollie (Dakar, Senegal)*

"I would like to take this time to thank you and your company for producing great and easy-to-learn products. I bought two of your books from a local bookstore, and it was the best investment I've ever made! Thank you for thinking of us ordinary people."
*Jeff Eastman (West Des Moines, IA)*

"Compliments to the chef!! Your books are extraordinary! Or, simply put, extra-ordinary, meaning way above the rest! THANKYOU THANKYOU THANKYOU! I buy them for friends, family, and colleagues."
*Christine J. Manfrin (Castle Rock, CO)*

Oct 04

# CREDITS

**Project Editor**
Sarah Hellert

**Acquisitions Editor**
Jody Lefevere

**Product Development Manager**
Lindsay Sandman

**Copy Editor**
Dana Lesh

**Technical Editor**
Allen Wyatt

**Editorial Manager**
Robyn Siesky

**Permissions Editor**
Laura Moss

**Editorial Assistant**
Adrienne D. Porter

**Manufacturing**
Allan Conley
Linda Cook
Paul Gilchrist
Jennifer Guynn

**Book Design**
Kathie S. Rickard

**Graphics**
Joyce Haughey
Barry Offringa

**Production Coordinator**
Maridee V. Ennis

**Layout**
Amanda Carter
Jennifer Heleine
Stephanie D. Jumper
Heather Pope

**Screen Artist**
Jill A. Proll

**Illustrator**
Ronda David-Burroughs

**Cover Design**
Anthony Bunyan

**Proofreader**
Melissa D. Buddendeck

**Quality Control**
John Greenough
Susan Moritz

**Indexer**
Ty Koontz

**Vice President and Executive Group Publisher**
Richard Swadley

**Vice President and Publisher**
Barry Pruett

**Composition Services Director**
Debbie Stailey

## ABOUT THE AUTHOR

Joe Kraynak has been writing and editing computer books and training manuals for over 15 years. Joe has a master's degree in English and a bachelor's degree in Philosophy and Creative Writing from Purdue University. Joe is dedicated to making computers and the Internet more easily accessible to the average user.

# HOW TO USE THIS BOOK

Google®: Top 100 Simplified® Tips & Tricks includes 100 tasks that reveal cool secrets, teach timesaving tricks, and explain great tips guaranteed to make you more productive with Google. The easy-to-use layout lets you work through all the tasks from beginning to end or jump in at random.

## Who is this book for?

You already know Google basics. Now you'd like to go beyond, with shortcuts, tricks, and tips that let you work smarter and faster. And because you learn more easily when someone *shows* you how, this is the book for you.

## Conventions Used in This Book

**❶ Steps**

This book uses step-by-step instructions to guide you easily through each task. Numbered callouts on every screen shot show you exactly how to perform each task, step by step.

**❷ Tips**

Practical tips provide insights to save you time and trouble, caution you about hazards to avoid, and reveal how to do things in Google that you never thought possible!

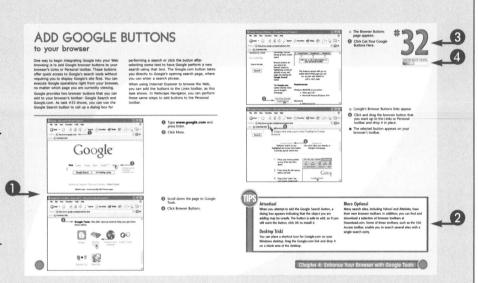

**❸ Task Numbers**

Task numbers from 1 to 100 indicate which lesson you are working on.

**❹ Difficulty Levels**

For quick reference, the symbols to the right mark the difficulty level of each task.

| DIFFICULTY LEVEL | |
|---|---|
| DIFFICULTY LEVEL | Demonstrates a new spin on a common task |
| DIFFICULTY LEVEL | Introduces a new skill or a new task |
| DIFFICULTY LEVEL | Combines multiple skills requiring in-depth knowledge |
| DIFFICULTY LEVEL | Requires extensive skill and may involve other technologies |

# Table of Contents

Google Directory - Recreation > Outdoors - Micros
File   Edit   View   Favorites   Tools   Help
Back   ·   ×   Search
Address   http://directory.google.com/Top/Recreation/Outdo

**Google** Directory   boundary w   ◉ Search o

**Outdoors**
Recreation > Outdoors

**Categories**

| | |
|---|---|
| Arrowhead | Hiking (645) |
| Collecting (49) | Horseback |
| Birding (2223) | Riding (6) |
| Boating (3949) | **Hunting** (3890) |
| **Camping** (3596) | Landsailing (23) |
| Canoe and | Letterboxing (35) |

Google Search: mount rainier - Microsoft Internet Explor
File   Edit   View   Favorites   Tools   Help
Back   ·   ×   Search   Favo
Address   http://images.google.com/images?q=mount+rainier&ie=UTF

**Google** Images   Web   **Images**   Groups   News
mount rainier
Moderate SafeSearch is on

**Images**   Results 1 - 20 of about **10,200** for

mount-rainier.jpg
273 x 337 pixels - 18k
www.basecamp.cnchost.com/
campersf.htm

rainier3.jpg
432 x 305 pixels - 48k
www.eskimo.com/~bpentium
rainier/rainier3.jpg

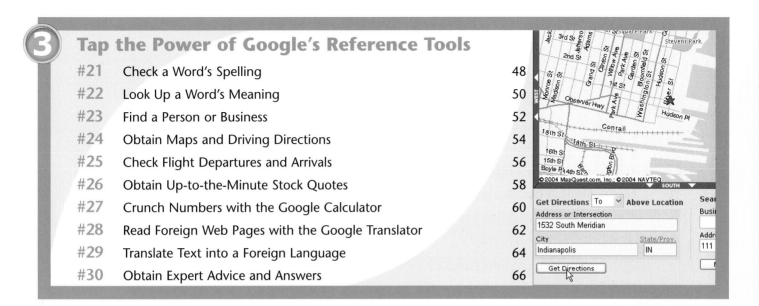

# Table of Contents

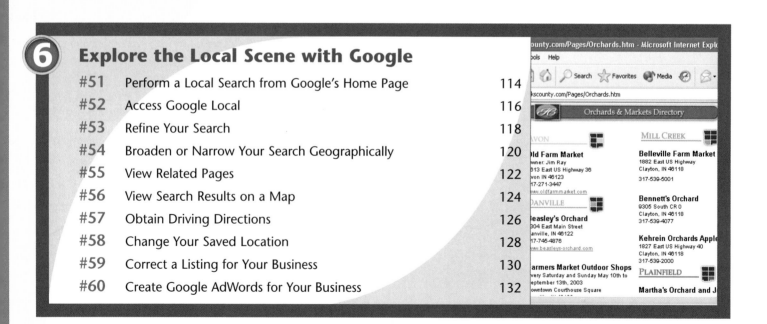

**5  Get Your News through Google News**

**6  Explore the Local Scene with Google**

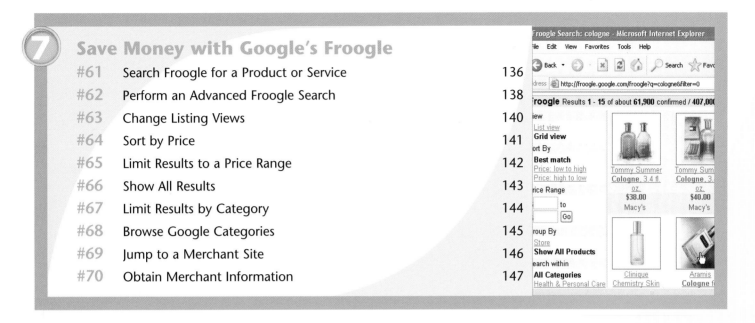

## 7 Save Money with Google's Froogle

## 8 Read and Post Messages in Discussion Forums

# Table of Contents

# Maximize Google Search Options

Google is a powerful search engine that millions of people use every day to find specific information and resources on the Web. However, most people do not exploit the full potential of Google's power. They open Google's home page, type one or more search terms, click the Google Search button, and then look through the list of links to see whether Google turned up any interesting pages. Many people do not realize that they may be looking at a list of ten links out of a million that matched their search entry!

Google is a much more effective search tool if you know how to use its various search features. By simply changing Google's startup preferences, for example, you can limit the list to a single language, such as English or Swedish, and screen out any sites that contain objectionable content. By understanding how to enter search operators, you can have Google deliver links to only those pages that contain an exact match of your search entry or only those pages that have your search entry in their title. And when you find a page that interests you, you can send Google to search for similar pages.

Because Google looks so basic when first viewed, users often overlook its many options and high-powered search tools. This chapter takes you behind the scenes, showing you how to customize Google, use Boolean search operators to narrow or broaden your search, enter special Google search operators, take advantage of the Google Directory, and much more.

# Top 100

# Customize search results with
# GOOGLE PREFERENCES

By default, Google displays the search results of all pages, regardless of language, and uses moderate content filtering to screen out any sites that may be inappropriate for children. Unless you specify otherwise, Google displays ten links at a time and displays them in the same browser window that you use to perform your search. The settings for these options work behind the scenes to control the way Google displays search results.

Most users do not change Google's default settings, either because they do not realize that they can

change them or because they are satisfied with the way Google displays the search results. However, you can target your searches by changing some of these preferences. For example, by displaying only those pages that appear in a specific language, such as English, you automatically filter out dozens of other languages from your search. You can also have Google omit links to sites that contain potentially offensive material by turning on SafeSearch filtering. This task shows how to enter your preferences.

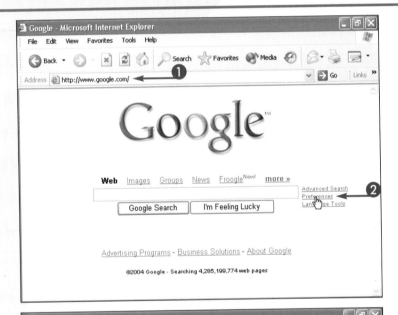

❶ Type **www.google.com** and press Enter.

❷ Click Preferences.

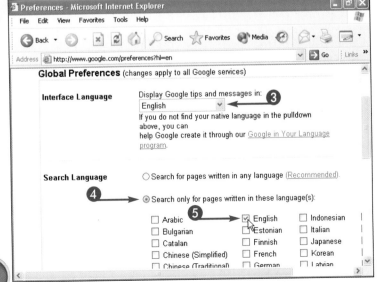

Google's Global Preferences screen appears.

❸ Click here and select the language in which you prefer to have results displayed.

❹ Click here to screen out pages in other languages.

❺ Click the option next to each language to include it in the search results.

4

**6** Scroll down the page.

**7** Click the SafeSearch filtering option that you want.

**8** Click here and select the number of results that you want Google to display.

**9** Click here to have search results displayed in a separate window.

**10** Click Save Preferences.

**DIFFICULTY LEVEL**

Google informs you that it has saved your preferences.

**11** Click OK.

You are returned to Google's home page.

### Attention!

To have Google save your preferences, your browser must accept cookies. Browsers typically accept cookies unless the user enters a setting instructing the browser to reject them.

### Did You Know?

If strict SafeSearch filtering fails to prevent an obscene site from turning up in a Google search, report the site to safesearch@google.com, and Google will investigate it.

### Did You Know?

If you share your computer with others and use Windows profiles to sign on, Google search preferences apply only to the user who is currently signed on. Each user must enter his or her own Google search preferences.

# Limit the results with an
# ADVANCED SEARCH

By design, Google's basic search returns the most hits possible. It searches Web pages for the word or words that you entered and displays links to the pages that contain at least one occurrence of each word you entered. The number of links Google returns typically exceeds any user's needs and often prevents users from finding links to the best sites in a particular category.

Fortunately, Google features an Advanced Search page that can help you focus your search and ignore many of the lesser sites. You can use the Advanced

Search options, for example, to search for only those pages that have your search word or words in their page title or search for only pages that Webmasters have updated in the last three months.

This task shows you how to use many of the more helpful options on Google's Advanced Search page for narrowing your search. You can also pick up some additional tips and suggestions for making your searches more focused.

**①** Type **www.google.com** and press Enter.

**②** Click Advanced Search.

The Advanced Search page appears.

**③** Type your search word or words in one or more of the Find Results boxes.

**④** Click here and select the number of links to display per page.

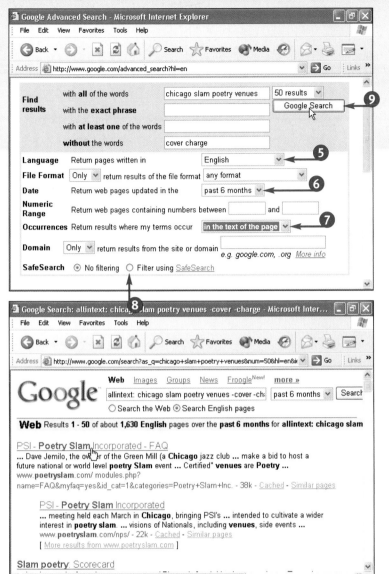

⑤ Click here and select the language that you want.

⑥ Click here and select the page update range.

⑦ Click here and select where you want Google to look for the words that you typed in step **3**.

⑧ Click an option to specify the level of SafeSearch filtering you want.

⑨ Click Google Search.

Google displays links to pages that match your search instructions.

**TIPS**

**Try This!**
Load Google's home page at www.google.com, type your search terms, and click the I'm Feeling Lucky button. Instead of displaying links to several sites, Google automatically routes you to the first site it would normally list in its search results.

**Did You Know?**
Google's Advanced Search form is a user-friendly way to perform advanced searches without typing search operators. In tasks #6 and #7, you discover how to enter the search operators directly on Google's opening screen to save time.

**Try This!**
Open Google's Advanced Search page and then use your browser's configuration settings to set the page as your browser's home page.

# Search a
# SPECIFIC WEB SITE

Many Web sites open with a search text box and button that enable you to search the site for specific information and resources. Other sites display a link that takes you to a search page that serves the same function. However, many sites do not offer the convenience of their own search engine. To find an item, you can browse the site by clicking links, but this often results in a futile search.

Fortunately, Google can help you search a site even if that site offers no search feature or index of its own. You can use Google to track down specific

information at a site by limiting your search to a particular domain. For example, you can have Google search www.foxmovies.com for "comedy" or "drama" or a specific movie title or actor's name.

You can search a domain name by performing an advanced search at Google and entering the specific domain that you want to search. You can also enter a general domain name, such as **.org** or **.edu**, to search only those domain types.

1 Type **www.google.com** and press Enter.

2 Click Advanced Search.

The Advanced Search page appears.

3 Type your search terms.

4 Click in the Domain text box and type the name or partial name of the domain that you want to search.

5 Click Google Search.

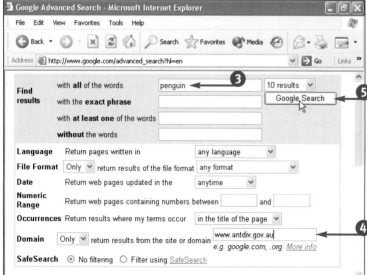

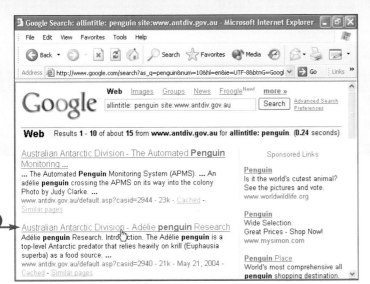

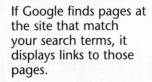

If Google finds pages at the site that match your search terms, it displays links to those pages.

⑥ Click a link that points to the content you want.

# 3

**DIFFICULTY LEVEL**

Your browser loads the page.

## Try This!

On Google's home page, click in the text box, type your search terms, type **site:** followed by the URL of the site that you want to search — for example, type **denzel washington site:www.foxmovies.com** — and press Enter. Google searches only the specified domain for the search terms that you entered.

## Try This!

Use the Domain option to omit domains or groups of domains from your search. For example, you may want to omit pages stored on commercial sites. In such a case, go to the Advanced Search page, click the Domain ⌄, and select Don't from the list. Then, click in the text box and type the domain type that you want to omit — for example, **.com**.

# Perform a
# TOPIC-SPECIFIC SEARCH

Google features topic-specific searches for commonly searched items. You can use Google's Government search, for example, to focus your search on U.S. Government and military sites or use the Universities search to search a specific college and university for information and paperwork that you may need. Google also features topic-specific searches for several technology sites, including Apple Macintosh, Microsoft, and Linux. These technology-specific searches can help you find technical support, updated software, and other information and resources that address your needs.

Google's topic-specific searches take advantage of Google's capability to search specific domains, as shown in task #3, but with topic-specific searches, Google displays a unique search page for the topic, making the search much more user-friendly and expanding it beyond a single domain.

Two of Google's topic-specific search tools are specialized to search for printed catalogs and a geographical location for information, products, and services. Chapters 6 and 7 cover these tools in greater detail. This task focuses on government, technology, and university searches.

❶ Type **www.google.com** and press Enter.

❷ Click Advanced Search.

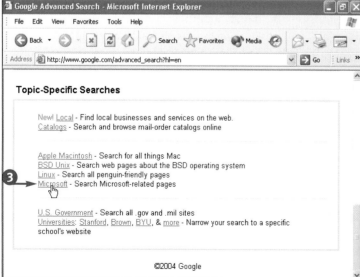

The Advanced Search page appears.

❸ Scroll down the page and click the link for the topic-specific search that you want to perform.

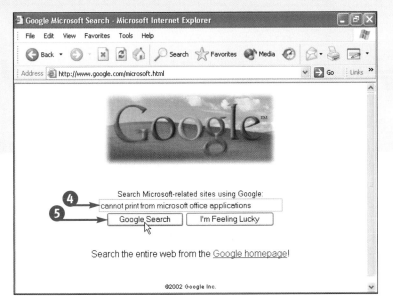

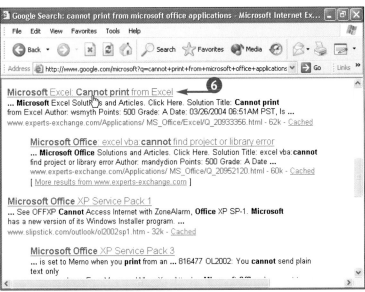

Google displays the selected topic-specific search page.

④ Type your search terms.

**Note:** *You can type Boolean or Google search operators to narrow or broaden your search, as shown in tasks #6 and #7.*

⑤ Click Google Search.

DIFFICULTY LEVEL

If Google finds sites that match your search terms, it displays links to those sites.

⑥ Click a link that may lead to the information you want.

Your browser loads the selected Web page.

## Did You Know?

When Google indexes a page, it stores a snapshot of the page as a *cached* page. The link you click opens the page to which the link currently points, which may be newer than the cached page and may no longer have the information you need. If you think the older page has the information, click the Cached link. Google does not cache all pages it indexes, particularly if a site's Webmaster requests that Google not cache the site's content.

## More Options!

Examine the search results carefully for additional options. For sites where Google finds more than one page that matches your search terms, it displays the More Results from *www.sitename.url* link, which you can click to view links to more pages at that site.

# Track down
# SIMILAR PAGES

When you perform a search, you often find a site that provides much of the content you were looking for but not enough to completely satisfy your needs. When this happens, most users return to the list of links and try clicking the next link in the list that looks promising. This hunt-and-click approach may deliver the results that you want, but it is not always the most efficient search method.

When you find a page that contains the content that you want, you can use that page to help track down

similar pages. By telling Google to find a page that is similar to the page you have already found, you give Google more information to target its search. Google can then return a list of links to pages that are more likely to contain the content that you need.

For many of the pages and sites that Google lists in its search results, it displays a Similar Pages link that you can click to search for pages that contain similar content.

**①** Perform a Google search as you normally would.

Google displays a list of links that match your search terms.

**②** Click the link for a page that looks promising.

Google loads the selected page.

**③** If the page contains the content that you want, but you want additional information, click Back.

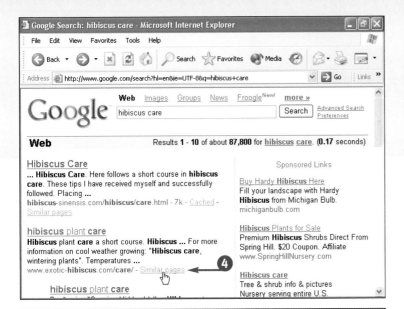

Your browser goes back to the search results.

④ Click Similar Pages.

**Note:** *Google does not display a Similar Pages link for all links that it displays.*

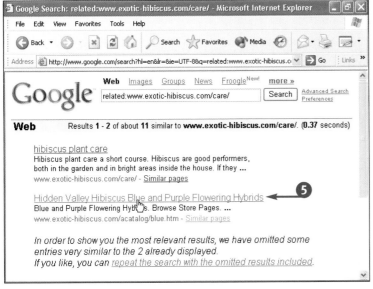

Google displays a list of links to similar Web pages.

⑤ Click the link for the Web page that you want.

Google loads the selected Web page.

## TIPS

### Did You Know?

To display similar Web sites, Google uses one of its search operators, as covered in task #7, to perform a new search. You can use the search operator yourself to find similar pages. Go to Google's opening page, type **related:** followed by the site's URL, and press Enter. For example, to find sites similar to www.imdb.com, type **related:www. imdb.com**, and press Enter.

### Try This!

To research competing companies or check out a competitor's products, search for the company or product and then click the Similar Pages link that appears below its link. This often returns a list of sites for comparable companies and products.

### Did You Know?

The Similar Pages feature may return a few links for highly specialized sites, such as personal Web sites.

# Master
# BOOLEAN OPERATORS

Almost all Internet search engines enable you to enter Boolean operators — AND, OR, and NOT — to phrase your search. In Google, you use "+," "OR," and "-". The "OR" must be uppercase, and you do not type the quotation marks. For example, you can enter the search phrase **baking +cookies -cakes** to find pages that contain the words *baking* and *cookies* but exclude pages that make any mention of cakes.

When you enter search terms in Google, Google assumes that you want to search for only pages that contain all of the terms you type. It assumes "and" is between each term. However, Google drops any

single letters from the search phrase and any common words, such as *the, who,* and *Web,* that slow down the search with no appreciable benefit. To force Google to include a word in the search, you can type a plus sign before the word. For example, to search for pages about Muhammad Ali, you can type **muhammad ali +the greatest**.

To broaden your search, you can insert "OR" between two or more search terms — for example, **baking cookies OR cakes**. A broader search returns a longer list of links.

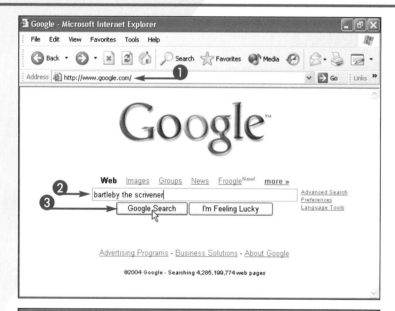

① Type **www.google.com** and press Enter.

② Type a search phrase that includes a word that Google is likely to omit from the search.

③ Click Google Search.

Google returns a list of links to pages that contain all your search terms.

④ Note the number of links found.

⑤ Type quotation marks before and after the title.

⑥ Click Search.

**DIFFICULTY LEVEL**

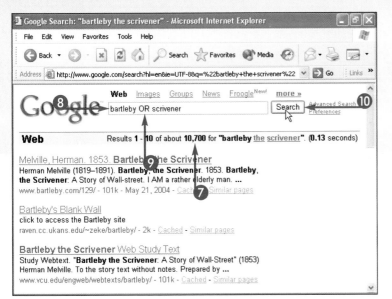

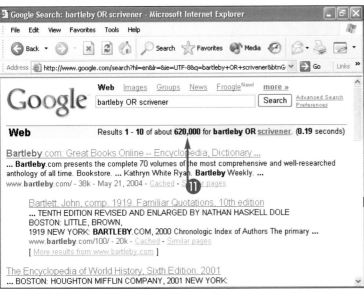

Google returns a list of links to only those pages that include the phrase exactly as you typed it.

⑦ Note the number of links returned.

⑧ Delete the quotation marks and any words that Google excludes from the search.

⑨ Type **OR** between the resulting words.

⑩ Click Search.

Google returns a list of links to pages that contain any one of the keywords in the title.

⑪ Note the number of found links.

The number of found links is greater because the search is much broader.

**Did You Know?**

The order in which you type terms in Google affects the search results. For example, **Pablo Picasso** and **Picasso Pablo** display somewhat different results. So be aware of the order in which you type your terms.

**Did You Know?**

If Google drops any words that you enter from its search, it displays those words directly below the text box near the top of the page, so you can see which words it omitted.

**More Options!**

Google enables you to search for sites that contain synonyms of the words that you type. To include a synonym, type a tilde (~) before the term; for example, to find sites that cover fitness, exercise, and related topics, you can type **aerobic ~exercise**.

Chapter 1: Maximize Google Search Options 15

# Master
# GOOGLE SEARCH OPERATORS

Google has a host of specialized operators, many of which it incorporates on the Advanced Search page. To save time, you can type the search operators when you perform a search.

Google's search operators include cache: to search only the snapshots of pages that Google indexes; link: to find pages that link to the specified page; info: to display any information that Google has about a site; define: to display a definition; stocks: to display a stock price; allintitle: to display sites that have all your search terms in their title; intitle: to

display sites that have the specified word in their title; allinurl: to find sites that have all your search terms in their URL; and inurl: to find sites that have the specified search term in their title. Task #3 includes coverage of the site: operator, which you can use to search a specific Web site, and task #5 discusses using the related: operator to find similar sites.

Some of these operators, including those that call for a URL, require you to omit any space between the operator and the entry that follows it.

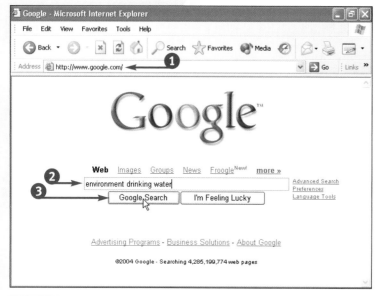

**1** Type **www.google.com** and press Enter.

**2** Type two or more search terms.

**3** Click Google Search.

---

Google performs the search and displays its results.

**4** Note the number of pages found.

**5** Click to the left of your first search term.

**6** Type a search operator to refine your search.

For this example, type **allintitle:** and a space before the first search term.

**7** Click Search.

## DIFFICULTY LEVEL

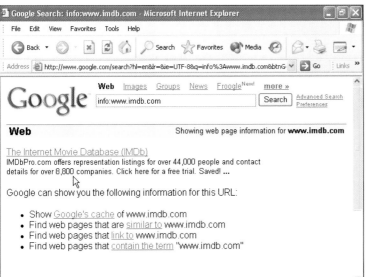

Google performs the search and displays its results.

⑧ Type another search operator to further refine your search.

For this example, type **info:** followed by the site's URL to find out information about a site.

*Note: Leave no space between the info: operator and the URL.*

⑨ Click Search.

If Google has any information about the specified site, it displays that information.

---

## TIPS

### Did You Know?

Many of Google's search operators have very specific rules that govern their use. For example, the intitle: operator can have no space between itself and the first word that follows it. Google finds any pages that have the first word in their titles plus any of the additional terms you typed in the body of the document. To learn additional details about the search operators, go to www.google.com/help/operators.html.

### Attention!

Leave no space between the search operators cache:, link:, related:, info:, and site: and the URL that you type after them.

### Did You Know?

You can combine Google's search operators with Boolean operators and quotation marks. For example, you can type **allintitle:"Vincent Van Gogh"** to find only those pages that have the exact phrase "Vincent Van Gogh" in their page titles. For more on Boolean operators, see task #6.

---

# Search for
# NUMERICAL RANGES

Most Google searches contain only words and phrases, but sometimes you may need to track down a product in a certain price range or some historical facts and figures for a range of dates. In these cases, users are often tempted to enter the range using a hyphen or the word *to* — for example, **1960-1972** or **$250 to $300**. As you might expect, these entries return erroneous results. Google treats the hyphen as a character to find pages that contain "1960-1927" or as a space to find pages that contain "1960" and "1972." If you use the word *to,* Google simply drops it from the search.

Fortunately, Google provides the numrange search operator for tracking down ranges of numbers. You simply type the two numbers of your range separated by two periods, with no spaces between the periods or the numbers — for example, **1960..1972** or **$250..$300**. Google recommends that for most ranges you enter a unit or provide some indication of what the range represents — for example, pounds, dollars, pixels, or miles.

**①** Type **www.google.com** and press Enter.

**②** Type your search entry, including the numerical range and the word **to**.

**③** Click Google Search.

Google displays the search results.

**④** Note that Google dropped the word *to* from the search.

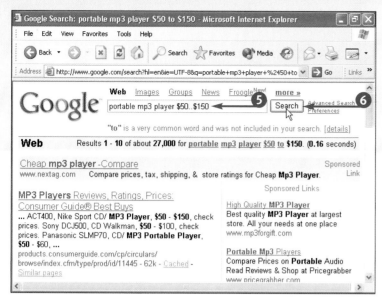

**⑤** Replace the word *to* with a pair of periods.

**Note:** *Leave no spaces between the periods or between the periods and the numbers that they separate.*

**⑥** Click Search.

**DIFFICULTY LEVEL**

Google performs the search using the specified numerical range.

**⑦** Note the difference in the search results that Google returns.

---

## TIPS

### Try This!
Type the same range using a hyphen rather than the numrange operator or the word *to.* Compare the search results with the results Google returned when you used *to* or "..".

### Try This!
Use the numrange operator along with a Google local search, covered in Chapter 6, to explore a range of local addresses. For example, if you want to see what is available along Sunset Drive from 900 North to 1500 North, add that range as **900..1500 north** to your search entry.

### More Options!
Numrange does not require a minimum or maximum number. You can search for a range of numbers up to a maximum number by typing the two periods before the number. Search beyond a minimum number by typing the two periods after the number.

# Maximize the power of the
# GOOGLE DIRECTORY

Because Google opens with its search page, many users overlook the outstanding Google Directory, which groups Web sites by category. In many cases, you can find better sites by following a trail of links in the directory rather than by searching for a specific site. Instead of searching Google for "Internet movie databases," which results in more than 3 million hits, you can go to the Google Directory, click Movies, click Databases, and find the top 13 or so movie databases on the Web.

To maximize the power of the directory, you can use

it in tandem with Google's search features. For example, you can navigate the directory to a particular category or subcategory and then enter your search terms to search only in that category or subcategory. You can also use the directory to find sites and pages that are similar to a site or page that you find useful.

This task shows you how to access the Google Directory and take full advantage of its features.

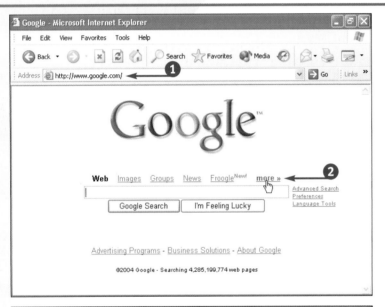

**1** Type **www.google.com** and press Enter.

**2** Click More.

The Google Services page appears.

**3** Click Directory.

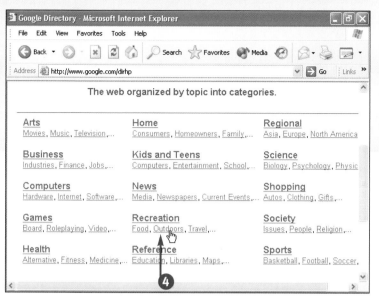

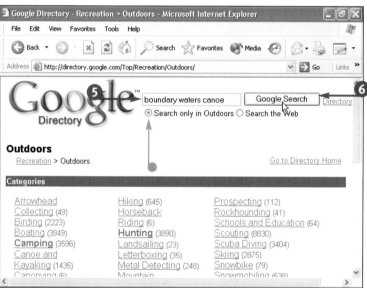

Google's main categories appear.

④ Navigate to the category or subcategory that you want.

Google displays a list of subcategories or sites in the currently selected category.

● The option to search only in the current category is selected.

⑤ Type your search terms.

⑥ Click Google Search.

If Google finds sites in the currently selected category that match your search terms, it displays links to those sites.

### Did You Know?

The Google Directory starts with sites selected and rated by volunteers as part of the Open Directory project. Google then uses its PageRank technology to determine the relative importance of a page. When you display a list of links in the directory, a green bar next to each link indicates its relative importance. You can access the Open Directory at dmoz.org.

### More Options!

When Google displays the links in a particular category, it displays one or more related categories just above the list of links. Click a related category to view additional sites that may contain relevant information.

### Try This!

Above the list of Web sites, click the View in Alphabetical Order link to arrange the sites by name from A to Z.

# Find pages that
# LINK TO A SPECIFIC PAGE

Google's related: search operator delivers a list of sites that contain content similar to that of a particular site. You can use Google's link: operator in much the same way to track down pages that contain links to a specific Web site or page. Of course, you have no guarantee that pages linking to a specific page contain related content, but the probability is fairly high. If you do find related information, it can help verify the information that you already found or expand on it, just like good cross-references in a book.

Web page authors can put the link: search operator to another use: to locate pages that link to their own pages. By performing a link: search using the URL of your own site, you can find out which pages, if any, link to your site. This is an effective way to determine potential Web partnerships. By performing a link: search using the URLs of potential partner sites, you can "network" to find even more potential partners and perhaps convince them to link to your site, as well.

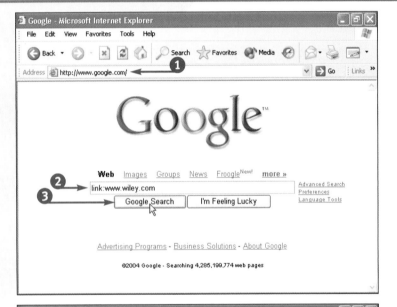

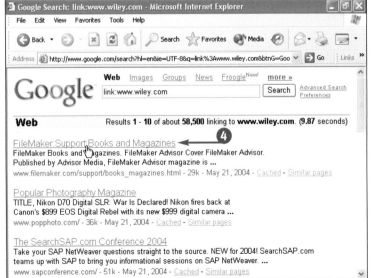

FIND LINKS TO A SITE

① Type **www.google.com** and press Enter.

② Type **link:** followed by the URL of the site.

*Note: Leave no space between link: and the URL.*

③ Click Google Search.

If Google finds pages that link to the site that you specified, it displays links to those pages.

④ Click a link to open the page.

Your browser displays the page.

22

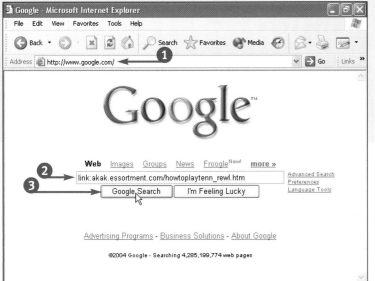

**FIND LINKS TO A PAGE**

① Type **www.google.com** and press Enter.

② Type **link:** followed by the URL of the page.

**Note:** *Leave no space between link: and the URL.*

③ Click Google Search.

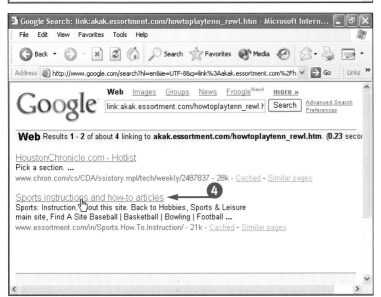

If Google finds pages that link to the page that you specified, it displays links to those pages.

④ Click a link to open the page.

Your browser displays the page.

**TIPS**

**Put It Together!**

Consider using the related: and link: search operators alternately to maximize the power of each. For example, you can use the related: operator to find sites related to a particular Web site and then use the link: operator on each site to find sites that link to the related sites.

**Did You Know?**

Google's Advanced Search page enables you to perform a related: or link: search. Go to the Advanced Search page, as shown in task #2, and scroll down the page to the Page-Specific Search options.

**Try This!**

If you perform a link: search to a specific page and Google returns no linked pages, delete the filename and directories from the end of the URL and do a link: search on the site's URL to broaden your search.

# Search for Images, Video Clips, and Other File Types

Google's Web search is, by far, its most popular feature, enabling you to search an index of billions of Web pages. However, you can search through much more than a Web page index. You can search for photos, clip art, illustrations, video clips, audio clips, and other types of files. Whether you want clip art images to add to your Web pages or you are looking for a wiring diagram, you can enlist the assistance of Google to locate the files that you need.

Google can track down specific files based on their *filename extensions* — the characters tacked on to the end of most filenames after the period — which identify the file type. Most Web page files, for example, end in the .htm or .html extension. Graphics files displayed on the Web commonly end in .jpg, .gif, or .png.

By searching Google for images rather than for Web pages, you can have Google retrieve only those common Web graphics file types.

Although Google does not provide a separate search option for audio and video files or other types of files, you can add filename extensions to your Web searches to focus your Google search on these specific file types. In addition to showing you how to search for graphics files, this chapter shows you how to locate audio and video files, PDF files, and Microsoft Office documents.

This chapter also shows you how to use Google's many search options and operators to focus and enhance your search of specific file types.

# Top 100

# Search quickly for
# IMAGES

Like its Web search, Google's image search offers a quick, basic search and an advanced search that enables you to set additional search options. Using image search, you can find clip art images, illustrations, diagrams, digital photos, and other graphics. Performing a basic search is shown in this task. Other tasks in this chapter show you how to use Google's advanced options.

Google's image index contains entries for millions of images stored on various servers all around the world. Google uses advanced search tools to locate

and index these images. Its search bot, a tool for surveying and indexing Web page content, actually searches Web pages that include images. It analyzes any text that is near the image, including the image caption, the name of the file, the URL that identifies the image file's location, and dozens of other clues to determine the content of the image. It then stores this information along with the location of the image file to help you in your search. Rather than having to search for an image by its filename, you can use a descriptive word or phrase to find the images you want.

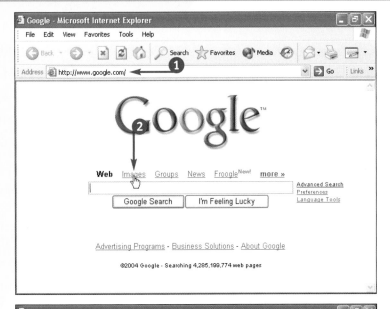

① Type **www.google.com** and press Enter.

② Click Images.

Google displays its Image Search page.

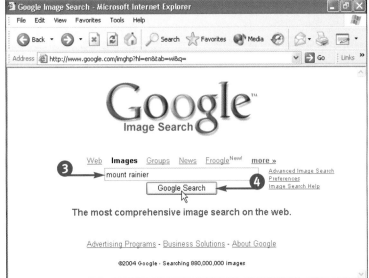

③ Type one or two words that describe the image that you want.

④ Click Google Search.

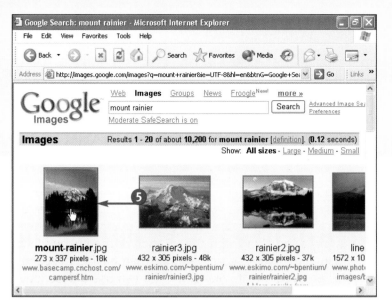

Google displays a thumbnail version of each image it finds that matches your search terms.

⑤ Click the thumbnail of the image that you want.

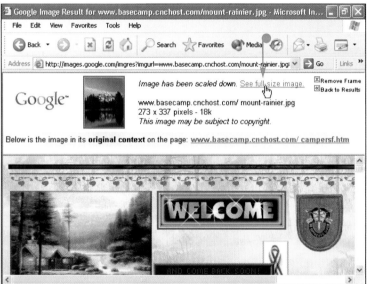

Google displays the image.

● You can click See Full-Size Image to view the image full size in its own window.

## TIPS

### Try This!
Instead of going to Google's home page first, go directly to images.google.com to perform your search.

### Did You Know?
When you click an image, Google displays a two-frame window. The top frame contains a slightly larger version of the thumbnail, which you can click to display the original image. The bottom frame displays the Web page that contains the image.

### Try This!
You can right-click an image in your browser to display a context menu with options for the image. You can save the image, print it, set it as your background or as a desktop item, or e-mail it. Most images are copyrighted, so do not distribute or reproduce an image unless you have written permission or the image is in the public domain.

# Search images of a specific
# SIZE OR TYPE

When you perform a basic Google image search, Google does as broad a search as possible, including images of every size and common type used on Web pages — JPG, GIF, and PNG. This results in the largest possible selection of images. However, it also results in images that range in size from tiny bullets to full-page photos. If you want to look for a detailed 4 × 5 or larger photograph of a tiger, for example, you may be a little disappointed to find hundreds of clip art images and photos the size of a postage stamp.

To filter out some images based on their size and type, you can perform an advanced search. For example, you can limit your search to large JPG files. Google features four size options: Any Size, Small, Medium, and Large. Large is typically 800 × 600 pixels or larger; small is approximately 50 × 50 pixels or smaller; and medium is everything in between. Google's advanced image search also enables you to search for full-color, black-and-white, or grayscale images.

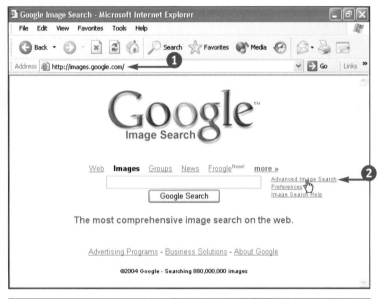

① Type **images.google.com** and press Enter.

② Click Advanced Image Search.

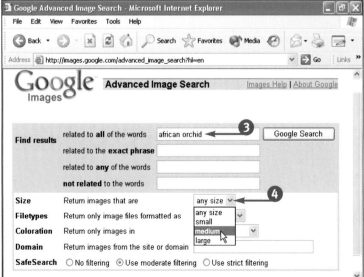

The Advanced Image Search page appears.

③ Type your search terms.

④ Click here and select the image size that you want.

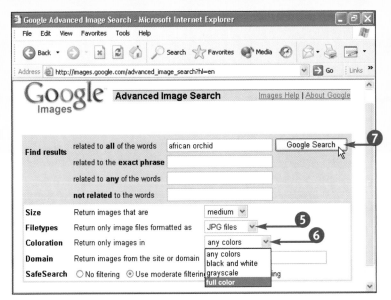

**5** Click here and select a file type.

**6** Click here and select the color option that you want.

**7** Click Google Search.

**#12**

**DIFFICULTY LEVEL**

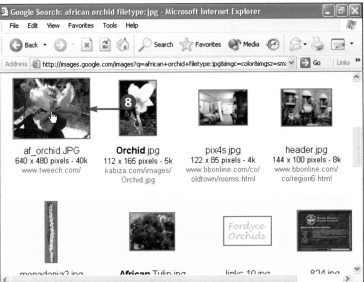

If Google finds images that match your search instructions, it displays larger versions of those images.

**8** Click the image that you want.

Google displays larger versions of the selected image.

## TIPS

### More Options!

In addition to specifying the image size, type, and colors that you want, you can type your search terms in any of the Find Results boxes to broaden or narrow your search. For example, you can type your search terms in the Exact Phrase box to find only those images whose associated text contains all the words you typed in the order that you typed them.

### Did You Know?

Google measures size by image dimensions. Although smaller images typically result in smaller files, other factors contribute to file size, including the file's format or file type, its resolution, and the number of colors it uses. A full-color photo, for example, is typically much larger than its grayscale counterpart.

# Track down images at a
# SPECIFIC WEB SITE

Most sites that feature collections of clip art, illustrations, and photos provide their own searchable index of images that is much more targeted than what Google can offer. However, some sites that are packed with images have few, if any, tools for searching their collections. If you want to use a particular image, you can spend hours going through pages and browsing through the collections and still never find the image.

Fortunately, Google provides an advanced search option that searches for images stored at a particular

site. As long as you know the site's address, or URL, you can enter it to have Google limit the search to the specified site. When you choose to search a particular site, Google adds its site: operator to the search entry to specify the site's URL. You can learn more about Google's advanced search operators in task #7. You can enter the entire domain name of the server, such as www.wiley.com, to narrow your search or enter a portion of the URL, such as .edu, to broaden it.

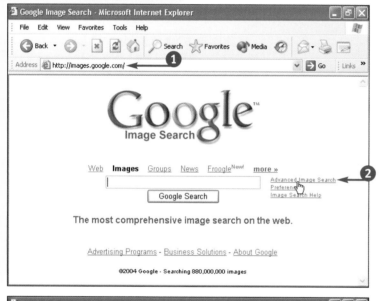

① Type **images.google.com** and press Enter.

② Click Advanced Image Search.

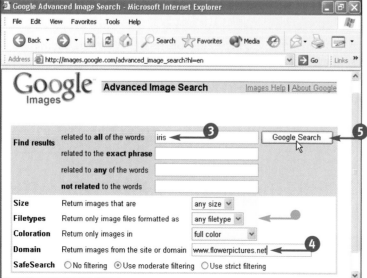

The Advanced Image Search page appears.

③ Type your search terms.

● You can select size, file type, and color options.

④ Type the URL or a portion of a URL to specify the location of the site that you want to search.

⑤ Click Google Search.

If Google finds images that match your search instructions, it displays thumbnails of those images.

● Note that Google limits the search results to the domain you specified in step **4**.

⑥ Click the thumbnail of the image that you want to view.

Google displays the image.

● You can click See Full-Size Image to view the image full size in its own window.

---

**TIPS**

### Did You Know?
Google's image search indexes more than 880 million images, but that represents only a fraction of the images stored on the Internet. Do not be surprised if Google does not find images on a particular site that you know are stored at that site. Google adds images to its index regularly in an attempt to be as comprehensive as possible.

### Did You Know?
Google attempts to screen out any duplicate images in its index to provide users with a collection of unique images. It also indexes photos and other images at many of the more popular news sites to keep its image index up-to-date with current events.

# Search using
# BOOLEAN AND GOOGLE OPERATORS

When you type two or more words to perform a search, Google assumes that you want to find images whose surrounding text contains all of those words, not necessarily in the order that you typed them. You can use Boolean operators and Google search operators to instruct Google on how to use your entries in the search. For example, instead of finding images related to lions and tigers and bears, you can type **lions OR tigers OR bears** to have Google find images that relate to any one of the typed entries.

Google's advanced search and advanced image search use Boolean and Google search operators behind the scenes to configure the search operation. If you type your search phrase in the Exact Phrase box, for example, Google searches for only those images whose surrounding text exactly matches the words you typed in the order in which you typed them. You could perform the same search by enclosing your search phrase in quotation marks.

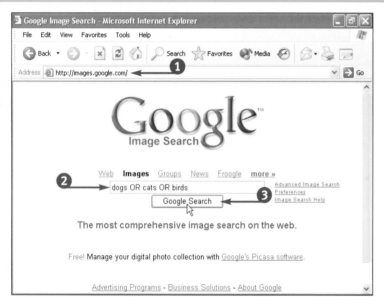

① Type **images.google.com** and press Enter.

② Type two or more words separated by the word **OR** to describe an image that you want.

③ Click Google Search.

Google displays thumbnails of any images that match your search instructions.

④ Delete OR from between each word in your search phrase.

⑤ Enclose your search phrase with quotation marks.

⑥ Click Search.

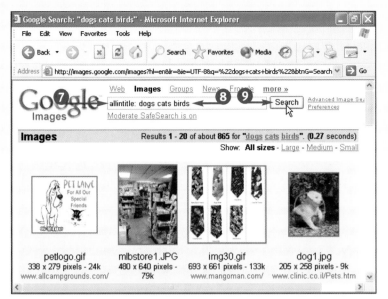

If Google finds any images whose surrounding text matches your search phrase exactly, it displays thumbnails of those images.

⑦ Delete the quotation marks.

⑧ Type **allintitle:** and a space at the beginning of the search phrase.

⑨ Click Search.

DIFFICULTY LEVEL

If Google finds any images on Web pages that have all the search words in their titles, it displays thumbnails of those images.

---

## TIPS

### More Options!

You can omit a word or term from your search phrase by typing a hyphen before the word. Do not include any space between the hyphen and the word. This tells Google to omit any images that have the word associated with it.

### More Options!

The operator for synonyms, the tilde, has no apparent effect on the number of results returned. You might expect a search for "~car" to turn up search results for "car" and "automobile," but the number of search results does not differ.

### Did You Know?

When you perform a search that results in images at news sites, Google displays thumbnails for those images at the top of the collection of thumbnails. Google does this to provide you with the most-recently published images first.

---

# REMOVE COPYRIGHTED IMAGES
## from the search

If you have your own Web site that includes images, those images are accessible to anyone who wants to view your page. They are also accessible to any automated search index, including Google. As Google's search bots scan the Web for new content, they are likely to add your site to Google's Web index and add any images on your pages to Google's image index. Google then displays your image as a result of any search a user performs that contains words relating to your images.

In most cases, you want users to visit your site and view its content — both its text and graphics. However, many people use a Google image search not only to view images, but also to copy and use them in their own publications — on the Web or in print. If you have artwork or photographs that are copyrighted and that you want Google to exclude from its index, you can create a text file that instructs Google's search bot to omit images. You can also submit a Google request to expedite the removal of your site from Google's search results.

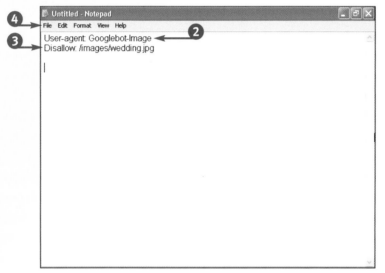

### USE A TEXT FILE

① Open a text file editor, such as Windows Notepad.

② Type **User-agent: Googlebot-Image**.

③ Type **Disallow:** followed by the path and filename of the image that you want to omit.

*Note: To remove all images, type **Disallow: /** and then a space.*

④ Click File.

⑤ Click Save.

The Save As dialog box appears.

⑥ Name the file **robots.txt**.

⑦ Click Save.

*Note: You must copy the file to the root directory of your Web server or have your site's Webmaster do it.*

Google's search bot will no longer add the specified image to the Google search index.

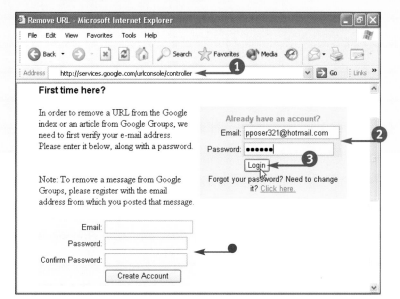

① Type
**services.google.com/ urlconsole/controller**
and press Enter.

● If you are not already registered on Google, register and log on to Google here.

② Type your e-mail address and password.

③ Click Login.

Google displays instructions on how to have your URL's content removed from the index.

④ Scroll down the page and follow the on-screen instructions to enter the URL that you want removed.

Google removes your images from its index in three to five business days.

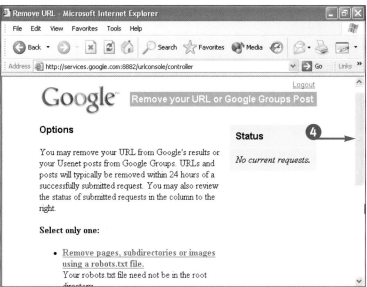

## Attention!

You can submit a request to have Google omit your images from its index for 90 days, but after this time, Google's bot may add your images back into Google's search index. To prevent Google from relisting them in the index, you must create the robots.txt file and store it in the root directory of the Web server.

## More Options!

Google provides many options for controlling the way it indexes and lists your site. You can have your entire site or selected pages removed from Google's index, change your site's URL, remove an outdated link, or remove pages stored in Google's cache, which stores a snapshot of each page it indexes. To learn how to perform these tasks, go to www.google.com/remove.html.

# Filter out
# ADULT IMAGES

By default, Google filters out most adult-content images from its results by using its moderate filtering setting. Unless you search intentionally for adult content, the results reveal little that most people would find offensive. However, moderate filtering does let some potentially offensive material pass through, especially if one or two search terms refer to such content.

You can change Google's content-filtering setting for all aspects of Google by adjusting your search preferences, as shown in task #1. These preferences

apply to all aspects of Google, including Web and image searches. Assuming that your browser has cookies enabled, it saves the preferences you entered. The content filter setting then controls the results that Google delivers.

You can use a different content-filtering setting for images whenever you perform an advanced search. At the bottom of the Advanced Search page, you can choose No Filtering, Use Moderate Filtering, or Use Strict Filtering.

① Type **images.google.com** and press Enter.

② Click Advanced Image Search.

The Advanced Image Search page appears.

③ Type one or more words to describe the image that you want.

④ Click Use Strict Filtering.

⑤ Click Google Search.

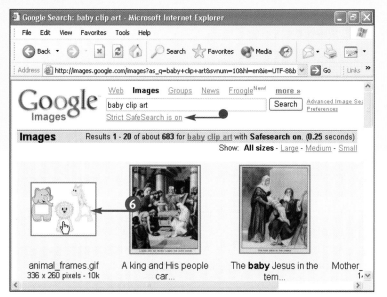

If Google finds any images that match your search instructions, it displays thumbnails of the images.

● Google displays the filtering option that is in effect.

❻ Click the thumbnail of an image to view a larger version.

Google displays a larger thumbnail version in the upper frame and the Web page that contains the image in the lower frame.

## TIPS

### Did You Know?
When you perform an advanced search of Web pages or images, the filtering option that you select on the Advanced Search page overrides the SafeSearch filtering option selected on the Preferences page. However, it does not change the setting on the Preferences page.

### Important!
If you are a parent or guardian of a young child who uses a computer, do not rely on Google's filtering options to completely block out any potentially offensive content. Even strict filtering can permit some offensive images and text. Supervise young children closely.

### Did You Know?
On the Preferences page, the Use Strict Filtering setting screens out offensive images and text. Use Moderate Filtering screens out only the most explicit images.

# Locate
# AUDIO RECORDINGS

Some of the most sought-after files on the Web are media files, including MP3 files and files stored in other popular file formats, including RA (Real audio) and WMA (Windows Media audio). You may find it difficult to locate a specific recording. Unfortunately, as of the writing of this book, Google has no audio search feature comparable to its image search.

Searching for audio files by name is not an option because, like most search engines, Google drops the period from any search phrase. You can try adding the filename extension to your search phrase, but

that often results in links to hundreds of commercial sites. Although Google features the filetype: operator to search for different document types, the operator does not function with audio file types.

To overcome these limitations, you can hack Google to display browsable directories that may contain the files you want. *Hacking* consists of making Google perform a task it was not designed to perform. The hack shown here instructs Google to display file repositories for common audio file types: AU, WAV, MP3, WMA, and RA.

---

❶ Type **www.google.com** and press Enter.

❷ Type a search phrase to describe the type of audio clip that you want.

**Note:** *If you are searching for a song, type the artist name or song title. Include +"index of" and +"last modified".*

❸ Click Google Search.

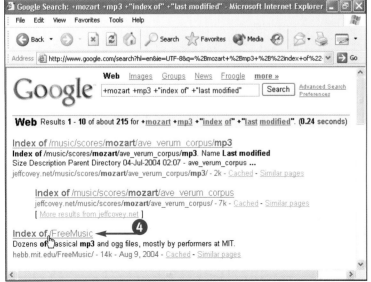

If Google finds any sites that list the song title, artist, or group that you specified, it displays links to those sites.

❹ Click the link to the directory that you want.

Your Web browser displays the contents of the site.

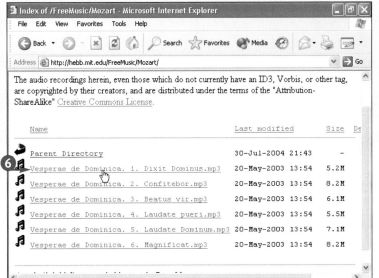

⑤ Follow the trail of links to the audio clip that you want.

⑥ Click the link for the audio clip that you want.

DIFFICULTY LEVEL

Your browser downloads the clip and starts playing it in the player associated with that audio file type.

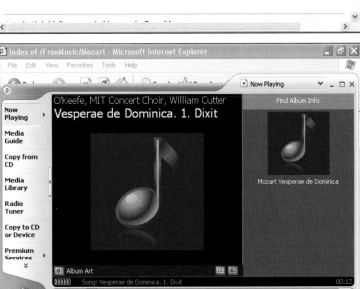

## TIPS

### More Options!

The example demonstrated in this task provides you with a search template that you can modify to search for other audio file types. For example, you can change +mp3 to +wma, +au, or +ra to search for files stored in other formats. Or you can replace the artist name with a song title.

### Did You Know?

When searching for audio clips, experiment with various ways of entering your search terms. For example, if you are searching for songs performed by a particular artist, try searching by last name only or by both first and last names. Try typing the first and last name as a single word or separating them with an underscore instead of a space. Also try transposing the names — last name first.

# Locate
# VIDEO CLIPS

Although MP3 and other audio file types are the most common, due to licensing issues, they are not necessarily the most accessible files. In many ways, video clips are more accessible, especially if you have a broadband connection capable of downloading large video files in a reasonable period of time. You can go to nearly any movie site and download a trailer and other teasers before or after a film release. In addition, hordes of independent filmmakers post their movies — or portions of them — on the Web, making them freely accessible.

However, if you do want to locate a specific video clip, a search engine can help. As of the writing of this book, Google does not offer a search tool specifically for video. However, a search for an actor, director, or unique movie title along with a filename extension of a common video file format, such as MPEG, often results in a few hits. Do not expect to find any full-length feature films, but you may find some of your favorite movie scenes.

① Type **www.google.com** and press Enter.

② Type a search phrase that describes the video content that you want.

   *Note: If you are searching for a movie clip, type the actor or director name or movie title. Include a video filename extension.*

③ Click Google Search.

If Google finds any sites that list the video content that you described, Google displays links to the sites.

④ Click the link to the site that you want.

   Your Web browser displays the contents of the site.

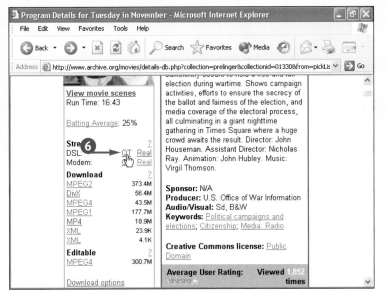

⑤ Follow the trail of links to the audio clip that you want.

⑥ Click the link for the video clip that you want.

Your browser downloads the clip and starts playing it in the player associated with that video file type.

This example shows QuickTime playing a movie clip inside the Internet Explorer window.

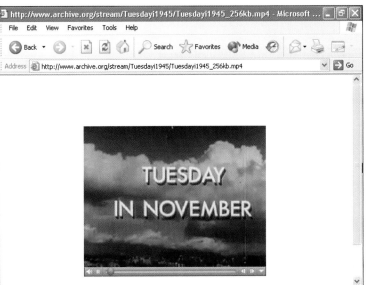

## More Options!

Although Google does not feature a special search option for tracking down audio and video clips, other search engines do. Try AltaVista at www.altavista.com or AlltheWeb at www.alltheweb.com or Singingfish at www.singingfish.com.

## Important!

If you try a Google hack like the one shown in task #17 to find video clips, the results often steer you to sites that feature adult content even if you search for a specific actor, director, or movie title. (A *hack* is an entry that causes Google to perform a task it was not designed to perform.)

## Did You Know?

Common video filename extensions are .mpg (.mpeg), .avi, and .mov. Try all filename extensions in your search.

# Locate
# PDF FILES

Many companies and government agencies publish and distribute documents as PDF, or Portable Document Format, files. PDF locks in the formatting of a document, so it appears the same when you display it on any monitor and when you print it on any printer. This makes PDF a very popular format for electronic publishing of eBooks and distribution of official forms.

The IRS, for example, makes all its tax forms available for downloading in the PDF format. Because

PDF locks in the formatting, when you print the form, it looks nearly identical to the form printed by the IRS.

When you search the Web using Google, Google looks for both HTML and PDF files. The list of links that Google displays contains files saved in both formats. Google provides a link that you can click to view PDF files in their native format, using Adobe Reader, or as Web pages, using your Web browser.

If you prefer PDF files, you can limit your Web search to PDF files using Google's Advanced Search page.

① Type **www.google.com** and press Enter.

② Click Advanced Search.

Google's Advanced Search page appears.

③ Type your search terms as you normally would.

④ Click here and select Adobe Acrobat PDF (.pdf).

⑤ Click Google Search.

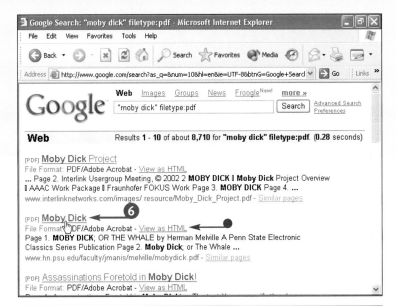

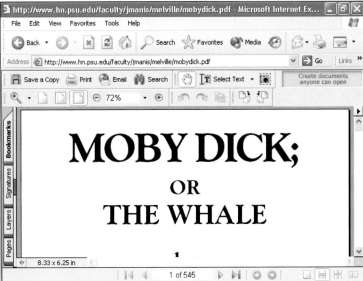

Google displays links to any PDF files that match your search instructions.

● You can click View as HTML to display the document as a Web page.

⑥ Click the link for one of the PDF files in the list.

⑦ Your browser downloads the PDF file and displays it in Adobe Acrobat Reader.

*Note: If Adobe Acrobat Reader is not installed on your computer, a dialog box appears, prompting you to save the PDF file.*

## TIPS

### Did You Know?

You can complete some PDF forms by typing in the blanks and clicking any check boxes rather than by printing the form and then filling it out by hand. Usually, if a site distributes forms that you can type on, it states this at the site.

### Try This!

Instead of going to Google's Advanced Search page, search for PDF files from Google's opening search page. Type **filetype:pdf** as part of your search phrase.

### Attention!

If Adobe Reader is not installed, you can download and install it for free at www.adobe.com or click the View as HTML link or View as Text link to view the document in your browser.

# Locate Microsoft
# OFFICE DOCUMENTS

Many companies and individuals use various Microsoft Office applications to create most of their documents. Increasingly, these same individuals and companies are placing these documents on their Web servers or FTP servers to make them publicly available. Because so many people have the applications required to view these documents, the authors see little need to invest additional time and effort into converting the documents into HTML format.

In the past, Microsoft Office documents remained relatively invisible on the Web because search engines ignored them. Now, Google includes these files in its standard search. If a link to a Word document appears in the search results, for example, you can open it in Word or view it as an HTML document in your browser.

In addition, you can limit your search to various Microsoft Office document types: Word DOC, Excel XLS, and PowerPoint PPT. You can also search for Microsoft Write WRI files; Microsoft Works WKS, WPS, or WDB files; and several other popular file types.

**①** Type **www.google.com** and press Enter.

**②** Click Advanced Search.

Google's Advanced Search page appears.

**③** Type your search terms as you normally would.

**④** Click here and select the type of Microsoft Office document that you want to search for.

**⑤** Click Google Search.

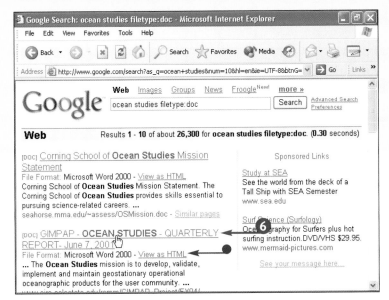

Google displays links to any Office documents that match your search instructions.

● You can click View as HTML to display the document as a Web page.

⑥ Click the link for one of the documents in the list.

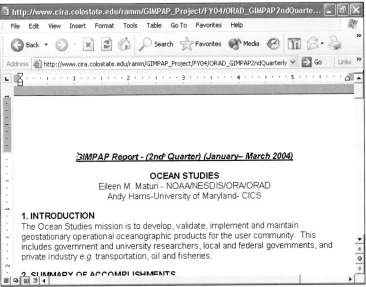

Your browser downloads the document and opens it in the appropriate Microsoft Office application.

**Caution!**
Google does not check documents for macro viruses or other potentially harmful computer code. Before opening a document, use an antivirus program to scan it. You can prevent infection by clicking the View as HTML or View as Text link.

**Try This!**
If you prefer to omit a particular file type from a Google search, use the filetype: operator to specify the type of file to exclude and precede it with a hyphen. For example, you would type **–filetype:pdf** to exclude PDF files from the search.

**Did You Know?**
When Google cannot identify the format of a particular document, it lists the document as Unrecognized. You can still view the document as an HTML or text file.

# Tap the Power of Google's Reference Tools

Google is much more than a search index. Google calls attention to misspelled search words and offers alternative spellings. It displays common dictionary definitions when you type a word or phrase. You can enter a company's ticker symbol to have Google fetch its current stock price. Google can find maps for addresses you enter, help check on flight arrivals and departures, and even translate pages written in a foreign language.

Google also features several operators that call reference tools into action. Using the define: operator, you can display a definition for a term or look up an acronym. Combine the stocks: operator with a ticker symbol, and Google displays trading information for the company's stock.

Google has many of these powerful tools built right into its search engine. If you carefully

observe the search results, you will notice that a Google search returns much more than a list of Web pages and links to sponsored sites. By turning your attention to the areas of the screen where Google typically displays these extras, you can make better use of Google's search results.

Additional tools hide behind Google's intelligent, though Spartan, interface. Did you know that you can enter a mathematical equation in Google and have Google display the answer? Did you know that you can enter a street address, complete with a zip code, to obtain a map of the area?

Many users never discover Google's many hidden talents. With this chapter, you find out just where to look.

# Top 100

# Check a
# WORD'S SPELLING

When you type a phrase and start a search, Google performs the search — no questions asked. If your search phrase contains a misspelled word, Google displays links to pages that contain the misspelled word. After all, many pages contain typos and misspellings, and you do not want those pages excluded from your search. Some pages, such as the Speeling & Grammer page (www.betterwords.u-net.com/speeling_&_grammer.htm), even contain intentionally misspelled words.

When you enter a search word or phrase, Google checks the spelling of every word that you enter and displays an alternative spelling for phrases containing typographical errors, misspelled words, or a word that has two or more correct spellings. Google then displays a link that you can click to perform the search using the alternative spelling.

In addition to executing accurate searches, Google's spelling feature provides a convenient desktop accessory for checking the spelling of individual words. Google bases its suggested spellings on all the words on the Internet, so Google often suggests alternative spellings that you may not find in a standard dictionary.

**1** Type **www.google.com** and press Enter.

**2** Type a search phrase that contains at least one misspelled word.

**3** Click Google Search.

If Google finds pages that contain the misspelled word, Google displays links to those pages.

**4** Note the number of pages that contain the misspelled word.

● Google displays your search phrase as a link with the corrected spelling.

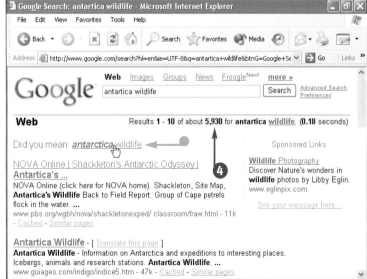

48

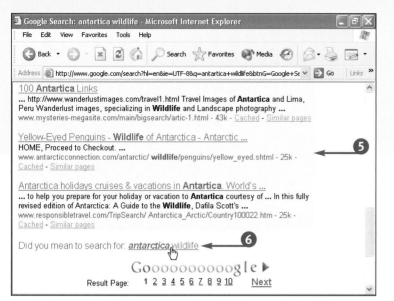

**DIFFICULTY LEVEL**

⑤ Scroll down the page and check the page descriptions to determine if these pages contain the information that you want.

Google repeats your search phrase as a link with the corrected spelling at the bottom of the page.

⑥ Click the link to perform the search with the corrected spelling.

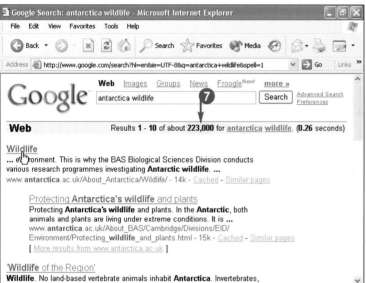

Google performs a new search using the correctly spelled word and displays links to pages that contain all the words in your search phrase.

⑦ Note the number of pages Google found with the corrected spelling.

*Note: Google typically finds more pages that contain the correctly spelled word.*

### Important!
Although Google does an excellent job of identifying possible misspellings, it may omit some alternative spellings. For example, if you search for "broadway theatre shows," Google may not offer "broadway theater shows" as an alternative. If Google does not identify an alternative spelling, perform two separate searches yourself.

### Try This!
If you know that a word has an alternative spelling, enter the search phrase using both spellings and separate the phrases with "OR". For example, you can type **broadway theater shows OR broadway theatre shows**.

### Try This!
To find additional pages on the Web, intentionally misspell words in your search phrase that people commonly misspell. Google may exclude pages that contain excellent information from a search simply because the creator misspelled a word.

# Look up a
# WORD'S MEANING

Dictionary Web sites, such as Dictionary.com and MSN's dictionary, enable you to look up the definitions for common words. When you research a topic with Google, however, visiting a separate dictionary site may be inconvenient. Fortunately, Google provides access to a comprehensive collection of definitions, making it possible to look up most words and phrases with a single click.

Google features several ways to access definitions. When you enter a word or phrase that has a common definition, Google displays a definition link just above the search results. You can click the link to display the definition. If you enter several words that each has a definition, Google displays each word as a link so that you can look up their definitions separately.

Google also offers the define: operator that you can type before a search word or phrase to have Google look up the definition for you or display a list of definitions from which to choose. Google's definition display varies depending on how you use the define: operator.

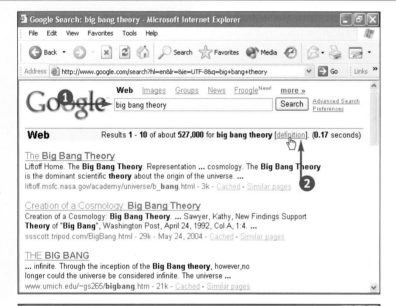

VIEW DEFINITIONS AFTER SEARCHING

① Perform a Google search as you normally would.

If Google finds pages that match your search word or phrase, it displays links to those pages.

② Click Definition.

*Note: If Google has a definition for two or more words in your phrase, it displays each word as a link that you can click for a definition.*

● Google connects to a definition site that displays a definition for the word or phrase.

① Type **define:** followed by the term for which you want a definition.

*Note: Leave no space between define: and the word or phrase.*

② Click Google Search.

**DIFFICULTY LEVEL**

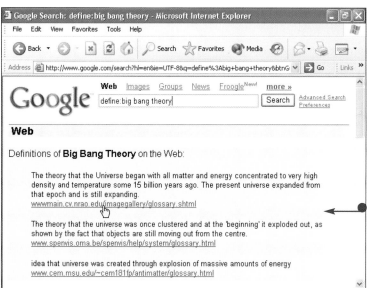

● Google displays one or more definitions for the word or phrase.

---

TIPS

## Try This!

Type **define** (no colon) followed by a space and the word or phrase for which you want a definition. Then click the Google Search button. If Google finds a definition for the word or phrase, it displays a link at the top of the search results that you can click to view a list of definitions.

## Did You Know?

When you click a search word or phrase in the band that appears above the search results, Google connects you to an online dictionary from which it obtained the definition.

## Did You Know?

When you use the define: operator to display a list of definitions, Google displays a link following the definition that you can click to display the Web page that contains the definition.

# FIND A PERSON
## or business

The Web features several sites devoted to helping users track down businesses and individuals. You can, for example, go to www.yellowpages.com to search for a business or visit www.whowhere.com to search for individuals or businesses. By entering a company name, you can often find its address and phone number. By entering an individual's last name, first name, city, and state, you can often obtain the person's residential address, phone number, and perhaps his or her e-mail address.

Google provides similar search tools. You need not click a link in Google to open a special page for performing the search. You simply enter the information you have about the business or individual and send Google on a search for the information you do not have.

If you enter a business name as your search phrase and Google has a phone book entry for the business stored in its index, it displays that information at the top of the search results. If you enter a person's name and zip code (or city and state), Google attempts to find and display the person's mailing address and phone number.

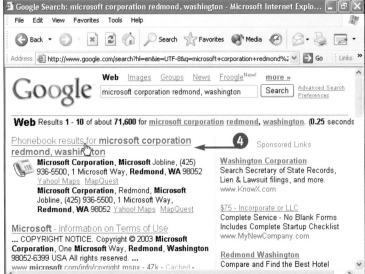

### SEARCH FOR A BUSINESS

❶ Type **www.google.com** and press Enter.

❷ Type the name of the business followed by its zip code, city and state, or phone number.

❸ Click Google Search.

Google displays phone book results for the specified business.

❹ Click Phonebook Results for additional listings.

Google displays a list of phone book entries complete with business names, addresses, and phone numbers.

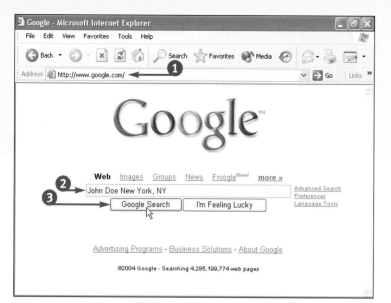

**# 23**

**DIFFICULTY LEVEL**

1. Type **www.google.com** and press Enter.

2. Type the information that you have about the person.

   *Note: You typically enter a person's first name or initial, last name, and city and state where the person resides, but you can search by phone number or zip code, too.*

3. Click Google Search.

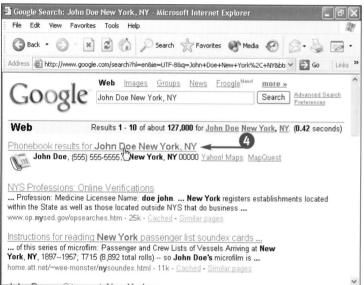

Google displays phone book results for the specified person.

4. Click Phonebook Results for additional listings.

Google displays a list of phone book entries complete with names, addresses, and phone numbers of people who match your search phrase.

**TIPS**

## More Options!

Type your search entries in one of the following formats: first name, last name, city, state; first name, last name, state; first name, last name, area code; first name, last name, zip code; last name, zip code.

## Did You Know?

Key terms trigger Google to perform a phone book search. If you enter a company name without a zip code, phone number, city, or state, Google does not display phone book listings.

## Try This!

Type **phonebook:** followed by a person's last name and the city, state, or zip code where the person lives, and click the Google Search button. Google searches its residential phone book and displays any listings that it finds. Try the same technique to track down businesses.

# OBTAIN MAPS
## and driving directions

When Google locates a residence or business, it often displays links to map services — such as Yahoo! Maps and MapQuest — where you can obtain a detailed map of the area. At these map sites, you can enter the address of your departure point to obtain complete driving directions that lead from the point of departure to the destination.

Although links to the map services appear when you search for a business or person, as shown in task #23, you need not search for a business or person to access a map. Entering a street address complete with a zip code or city name is often sufficient. In some cases, you may need to specify a state name, as well.

If you are looking for a more general map of an area, you can omit the street name and simply type a city and state or type the area's zip code. Then, after the map appears, you can zoom in on the area that you want.

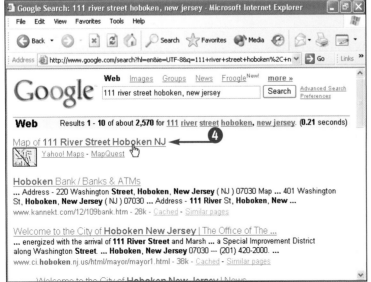

### GET A MAP

1. Type **www.google.com** and press Enter.

2. Type the address that you want the map service to map for you.

3. Click Google Search.

Google displays the Map Of link to the address that you entered.

4. Click Map Of.

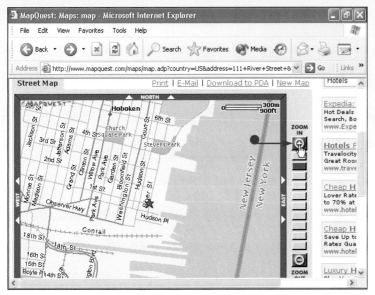

## 24

The map service displays a map of the area.

● You can use the controls at the map service to zoom in or out on the map.

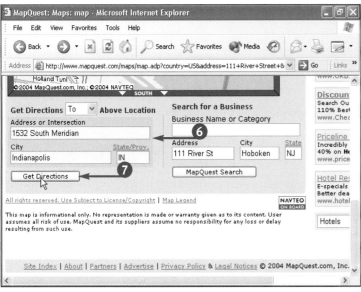

**GET DRIVING DIRECTIONS**

⑤ Scroll down the page.

⑥ Type the address, city, and state that defines your point of departure.

⑦ Click Get Directions to obtain driving directions.

The map service provides driving directions from the point of departure to the destination.

## Try This!

For a general map of a particular area, enter only the zip code. If you try entering the zip+4 digit postal code, such as "46224-5050," Google assumes that you want to perform a mathematical calculation and subtracts the second number from the first.

## More Options!

When Google locates an address, it may also display a phone book entry for the address and provide Google Local's listing for the address. See Chapter 6 for information on Google Local.

## Did You Know?

Google chooses map services based on their quality, not on any business relationships it has with these sites. At the writing of this book, Google used MapQuest and Yahoo! Maps, but Google may refer you to different map services.

# CHECK FLIGHT DEPARTURES
## and arrivals

Many airlines have their own Web sites, where you can check flight arrival and departure times. Airports may have their own sites, as well, where you can check the current weather conditions and find out if the airport is experiencing any delays. One of the better sites to check this information is www.flightarrivals.com.

However, with Google's assistance, you need not visit a special site to obtain flight information. Google can deliver all the information you need, assuming that you know how to enter your request. When you supply an airline name and flight number, Google

delivers current information on the flight's various departure and arrival times. If you supply an airport's three-letter code, Google delivers information about current weather conditions and any delays.

The information that Google delivers is not something it keeps track of itself. Google acts as a referral service, sending you to other sites that provide the information. For example, Google may send you to Travelocity for flight information or to the FAA (Federal Aviation Administration) site for airport weather conditions and delays.

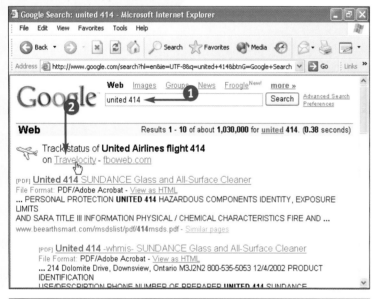

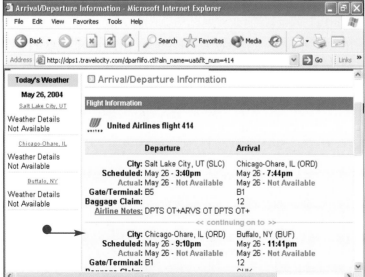

CHECK FLIGHT ARRIVALS AND DEPARTURES

① Perform a Google search using the airline name and flight number.

Google displays links to flight information sites.

② Click the link for the flight information site that you want.

Google connects to the flight information site and enters the information for you.

● The flight information site displays information about the specified flight, including departure and arrival times.

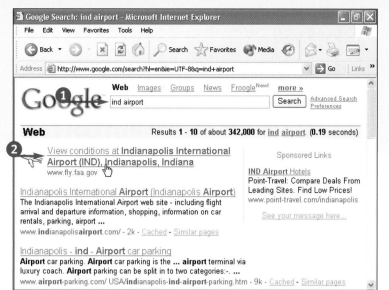

**1** Perform a Google search using the airport's three-letter code followed by **airport**.

Google displays a link to the site where you can obtain information about the specified airport.

**2** Click the link for the airport information.

**DIFFICULTY LEVEL**

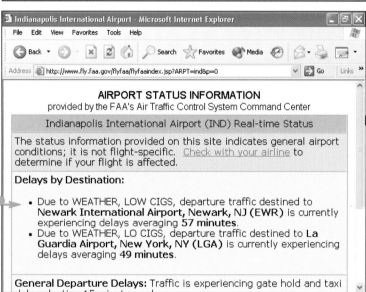

● Google connects to the FAA site, which displays weather conditions and information about any delays at the specified airport.

## TIPS

### Did You Know?
To check the current weather conditions and possible flight delays, you must have the three-letter airport code, which you can find at www.airnav.com/airports/. You can browse by state and city or search for a specific airport by name.

### Important!
The "three-letter" character code is not always three-letters; it can include numbers, as well. Also, airport codes may consist of more than three characters. If you encounter a four-letter code, such as KPHX, try omitting the first character when you type it in Google.

### Did You Know?
Google often includes news articles in its search. If you search for airport information, Google may return a link to one or more news articles that report on a certain incident at or near the airport.

# Obtain up-to-the-minute
# STOCK QUOTES

Whether you invest in individual stocks or in mutual funds, you may want to check on current share prices occasionally to determine how well your shares are doing. If you use special software to track your portfolio or you keep your portfolio information online, you can check all share prices in one location. However, you can use Google to quickly check share prices and research various companies.

When you enter a ticker symbol for a mutual fund or for a stock listed on the NYSE, AMEX, or NASDAQ

indexes, Google provides a link at the top of the search results that you can click to obtain the current stock price along with other financial data about the company.

Google does not provide the information itself, but connects you to several quality financial information sites. When you click a link for a stock symbol, the window that appears contains tabs to several financial information services. You can quickly check out the information from each service and compare it.

① Type **www.google.com** and press Enter.

② Type the ticker symbol for the company that you want to research.

*Note: You can look up ticker symbols at many sites, including money.cnn.com.*

③ Click Google Search.

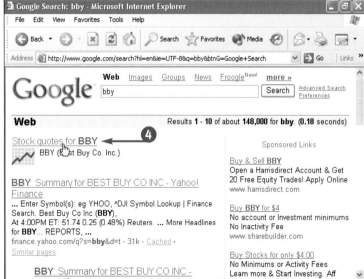

Google displays links to pages that contain the ticker symbol you typed.

④ Click Stock Quotes.

Google connects you to a financial information site, which displays the stock information.

⑤ To view additional information about this stock, click a tab for one of the other financial information services.

● The selected financial information service displays the information that it has available for this stock.

## Did You Know?

If you search for a company by name instead of ticker symbol, the Stock Quotes link may or may not appear above the list of search results. However, on the last line for the listing of the company's home page, Google displays "Stock Quote:" followed by the ticker symbol for that company. Click the link to view the stock price and other financial information.

## Try This!

Go to Google, type **stocks:** followed by a ticker symbol and click Google Search. Instead of displaying the Stock Quotes link, Google takes you right to a financial information page.

## Try This!

Type **stocks:** followed by two or more ticker symbols to have Google display quotes for each ticker symbol you typed.

# Crunch numbers with the
# GOOGLE CALCULATOR

Many users are unaware that Google's search page doubles as a fairly powerful calculator. Google can perform addition (+), subtraction (-), multiplication (*), division (/), and exponentiation (^); calculate percentages (%); determine square roots (sqrt); and more. Google can even work with trigonometric functions, including sine and cosine.

When you enter a series of numbers along with mathematical operators, Google attempts to perform the equation in a logical manner without requiring you to enter the equation in any special syntax. However, Google does follow the standard order of operations. It performs multiplication and division first and then addition and subtraction. So if you want to determine the result when you add 2 plus 2 and multiply the total by 5, you enter **(2+2)*5** to receive a result of 20. Entering **2+2*5** results in an answer of 12.

When you enter an equation, Google displays not only the result but also its interpretation of the equation. So if Google does not group expressions as you intended, you can correct the equation and have Google determine the new result.

**1** Type **www.google.com** and press Enter.

**2** Type your mathematical equation.

**3** Click Google Search.

● Google displays the equation that it performed, followed by the result.

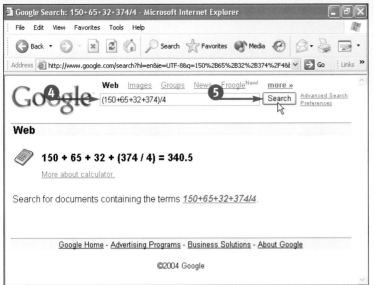

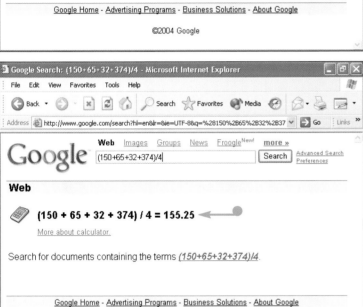

④ If Google grouped the mathematical operations differently than you intended, type parentheses to change the grouping.

⑤ Click Search.

● Google performs the calculation and displays the equation followed by its result.

## More Options!
Using a handful of mathematical operators along with the parentheses, you can perform the most common calculations. For additional operators and the recommended syntax for entering them, go to www.google.com/help/calculator.html. Google provides a table of mathematical operators along with examples.

## Important!
If Google identifies a mathematical operation as a phone number or address, it does not display a result. Type an equal sign (=) at the end of the equation to force Google to display a result.

## More Options!
You can convert units of measure by using the "in" operator. For example, type **10 kilometers in miles** to determine how many miles you ran in your last 10-kilometer race. Type **4 liters in gallons** to determine how many gallons of water you drank.

# Read foreign Web pages with the
# GOOGLE TRANSLATOR

Unless you specify that Google show links to only pages written in a particular language, as explained in task #1, Google's search results often contain pages from all over the world in many different languages. If you know the language, you can click the link and proceed to read the page. If you do not know the language, Google can possibly translate it for you, at least well enough so that you can obtain a basic understanding of it.

Google uses machine translation technology, which can perform rudimentary translations of non-English sites into English. At the writing of this book, Google could translate pages published in Italian, French, Spanish, German, and Portuguese.

If Google's search results include pages composed in any of these languages, Google displays a link for translating the page into English. If you click a link on the translated page that opens another page at the site, Google translates that page, too.

**1** Type **www.google.com** and press Enter.

**2** Type a search phrase that is likely to display links to Web sites in a foreign language.

**3** Click Google Search.

If Google locates any foreign language sites that include the words you typed, it includes links to them in the search results.

**4** Click Translate This Page.

Google translates as much of the page as possible.

⑤ Click a link that points to another page at the site.

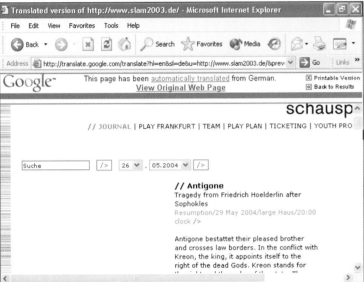

Google translates the linked page as well.

**TIPS**

## More Options!
You can return to the page in its original language by clicking the View Original Web Page link that Google displays just above the translated page. Also above the translated page and to the right are links for viewing a printable version of the page and for returning to Google's search results.

## Did You Know?
Google uses automatic translation technology that does not enlist the assistance of human translators. Due to the limitations of this technology, the translations are not perfect.

## Did You Know?
You can limit Google's search to a specific foreign language by performing an advanced search, as shown in task #2.

# TRANSLATE TEXT
## into a foreign language

Although Google can translate pages on-the-fly, Google features a collection of much more powerful translation tools on its Language Tools page.

Google's Language Tools page organizes the tools into four distinct areas. At the top of the page, you can search for Web pages in 35 languages stored on Web servers in more than 60 countries. Below that, you can type text in any supported language and have Google translate the text into another supported language. Or you can enter a Web page

URL and have Google open and translate that page. In the third area, you can choose the language that you prefer Google to use for its interface. Finally, near the bottom of the page, you can click links to dozens of other Google search sites around the world.

Of course, Google does not support all languages, but it can translate English, Italian, French, Spanish, German, and Portuguese. Google's powerful search tools combined with its translation tools make Google a truly global search index.

① Type **www.google.com** and press Enter.

② Click Language Tools.

Google displays the Language Tools page.

③ Scroll down to the Translate box.

④ Type the text that you want Google to translate.

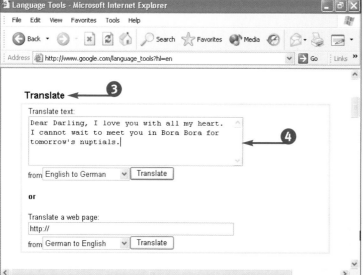

64

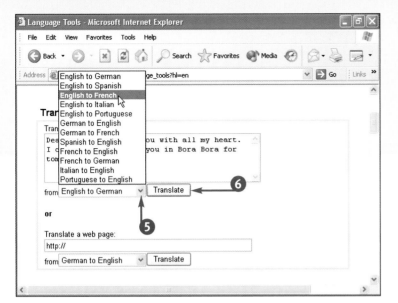

**DIFFICULTY LEVEL**

⑤ Click here and select the languages to translate from and to.

⑥ Click Translate.

● Google translates the text into the selected language.

**TIPS**

## Try This!

If you receive an e-mail message composed in a foreign language that Google supports, copy its contents and paste it into Google's Translate text box. Select the from and to languages and click the Translate button to have Google translate the message for you.

## More Options!

If you are searching for sites that are probably located in a foreign country, scroll down the Language Tools page to the area labeled Visit Google's Site in Your Local Domain. Click the flag that links to the Google search site in the country that you want.

## Try This!

When selecting the language that you want for the Google interface, read through the list carefully. Some of the options will have you laughing, such as Pig Latin.

# OBTAIN EXPERT ADVICE
## and answers

When you have a question that nobody seems willing or able to answer, where do you go to have it answered? You could try searching the Web, looking it up in an encyclopedia or other reference book, asking a librarian, or posting it in a newsgroup, but sometimes such quests for knowledge reveal less than you might hope.

Google provides a service where you can find expert answers to questions that other users have posted. Although a user must pay to have one of Google's expert researches answer a question, Google makes

the answers publicly available. You can search for the answer on Google's answer page, as shown in this task.

If Google's expert researches have not yet answered the question, you can post it at Google, specify how much you are willing to pay to have it answered ($2 to $200), and submit it. Google charges you 50 cents to post the question. Depending on the difficulty of the question and the amount you are willing to pay, one of Google's researchers usually delivers the answer in a matter of days.

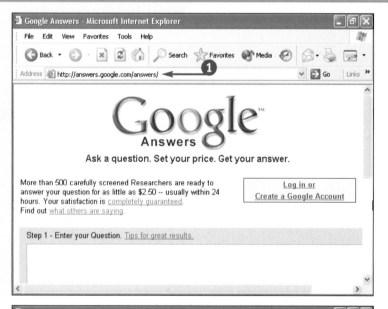

① Type **answers.google.com** and press Enter.

Google displays the Google Answers page.

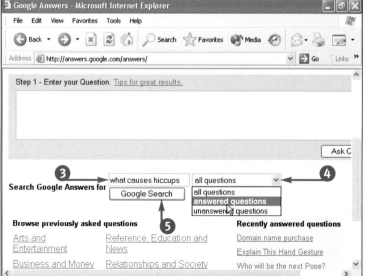

② Scroll down to the Search Google Answers For text box.

③ Type one or more words that describe the answer you are looking for.

④ Click here and select Answered Questions.

⑤ Click Google Search.

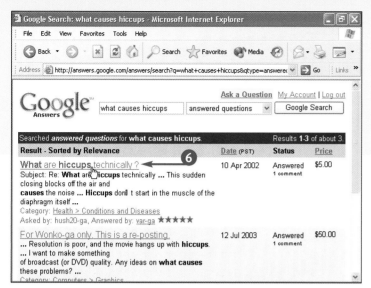

Google displays links to any questions that have the words you typed.

⑥ Click the link for a question that may have the answer that you need.

**DIFFICULTY LEVEL**

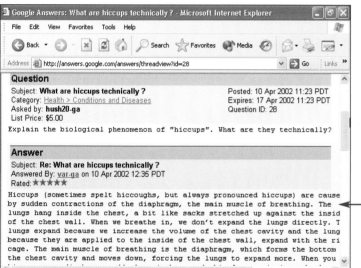

● Google displays the answer that the researcher posted.

## Did You Know?

To post a question, you must create a Google account with a valid e-mail address and password. You can create an account without entering any payment information, such as a credit card number. However, when you post your question, Google prompts you to enter payment information.

## Important!

If you post a question, be very specific and avoid questions that require multiple answers. Vague questions often go unanswered.

## Did You Know?

When you post a question, Google locks the question for four hours to give a researcher time to answer it. If the first researcher fails to answer the question in four hours, Google unlocks the question to give another researcher the opportunity to answer it. Google locks more expensive questions for eight hours.

# Enhance Your Browser with Google Tools

You can make Google a more integral part of your Web-browsing experience by accessorizing your Web browser with a selection of Google tools. Google provides buttons that you can add to your browser's Links or Personal toolbar. Google also offers the Google toolbar, which adds a Google Search box to your browser along with buttons for accessing Google News, highlighting search words in a document, and automating data entry on forms. Even better, the toolbar includes a built-in pop-up blocker to keep you from being inundated with unsolicited advertisements every time that you open a new page.

In this chapter, you learn where to find Google's powerful browser accessories and

how to add them to your browser. You learn how to highlight a word or phrase on any Web page and instantly search for it on Google. You learn the benefits of searching from the Google toolbar and how to use the toolbar to highlight all occurrences of a word on a page. And if you are tired of filling out forms online, you learn how to set up Google's AutoFill feature to fill in the blanks for you.

Even with Google's powerful accessories, you may not be surfing the Web as efficiently as possible, so this chapter also shows you how to customize Google's accessories to make them work even better for you.

# Maximize your
# LINKS OR PERSONAL TOOLBAR

Google provides two buttons that you can add to your browser's toolbar: Google Search and Google.com. The Google Search button calls up a box in which you can enter your search words. You can also use the Google Search button, as shown in task #33, to execute a search using selected words from any Web page. The Google.com button takes you directly to Google's opening search page, where you can perform a search as you normally do.

In Internet Explorer, you can add the buttons to the Links toolbar, which typically appears above the Web page viewing area. You can drag links from Web

pages and drop them on the toolbar to create buttons that enable you to quickly return to your favorite pages. Netscape Navigator calls its comparable toolbar the Personal toolbar, and it functions the same way: You drag links from pages up to the toolbar to create buttons. The Links and Personal toolbars are fairly small and can quickly become cluttered.

This task shows you how to make sure that the Links or Personal toolbar is visible and that it has space for your new buttons.

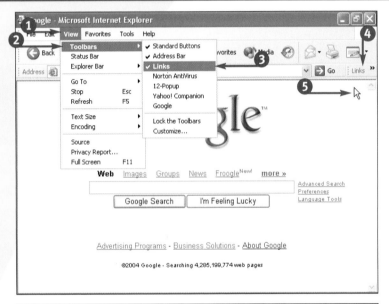

### PREPARE THE LINKS TOOLBAR

1. Click View.

2. Click Toolbars.

3. Click Links so that a check appears next to it.

4. If the Links toolbar is not showing, click and hold Links.

5. Drag Links down below the other toolbars and drop it in place.

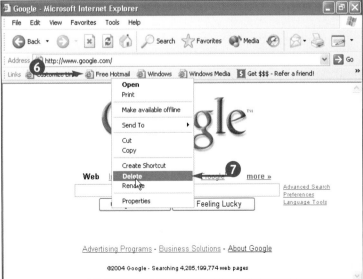

6. Right-click a link button that you do not use.

7. Click Delete.

    A confirmation dialog box appears.

8. Click Yes.

    Internet Explorer removes the button.

9. Repeat steps 6 to 8 to remove additional buttons.

    The Links bar is now maximized and has room for new buttons.

PREPARE THE PERSONAL
TOOLBAR

1 Click View.

2 Click Show/Hide.

3 Click Personal Toolbar so that a check appears next to it.

The Personal toolbar appears just below the Navigation Toolbar.

**DIFFICULTY LEVEL**

4 Right-click a link button that you do not use.

5 Click Delete.

Netscape Navigator removes the button.

6 Repeat steps 4 and 5 to remove additional buttons until you have space for at least two buttons.

The Personal toolbar is now maximized and has room for at least two new buttons.

**TIPS**

## More Options!

Instead of dragging Links down to place it on a line of its own, consider dragging it up to the menu bar and dragging it left to take up the free space in the menu bar. This leaves you with more space for viewing Web pages.

## More Options!

You can rearrange links on the Links or Personal toolbar by dragging them from their current position to a new position on the toolbar. When you drag a link to the left or right of another link, a vertical line appears showing the link's new position. Release the mouse button to drop the link in place.

# ADD GOOGLE BUTTONS
## to your browser

One way to begin integrating Google into your Web browsing is to add Google browser buttons to your browser's Links or Personal toolbar. These buttons offer quick access to Google's search tools without requiring you to display Google's site first. You can execute Google operations right from your browser, no matter which page you are currently viewing.

Google provides two browser buttons that you can add to your browser's toolbar: Google Search and Google.com. As task #33 shows, you can use the Google Search button to call up a dialog box for

performing a search or click the button after selecting some text to have Google perform a new search using that text. The Google.com button takes you directly to Google's opening search page, where you can enter a search phrase.

When using Internet Explorer to browse the Web, you can add the buttons to the Links toolbar, as this task shows. In Netscape Navigator, you can perform these same steps to add buttons to the Personal toolbar.

① Type **www.google.com** and press Enter.

② Click More.

③ Scroll down the page to Google Tools.

④ Click Browser Buttons.

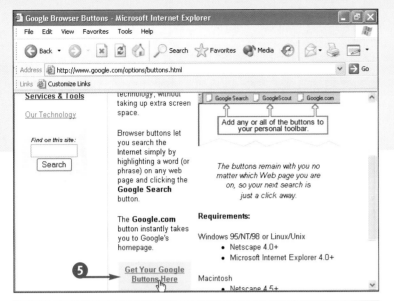

The Browser Buttons page appears.

⑤ Click Get Your Google Buttons Here.

**DIFFICULTY LEVEL**

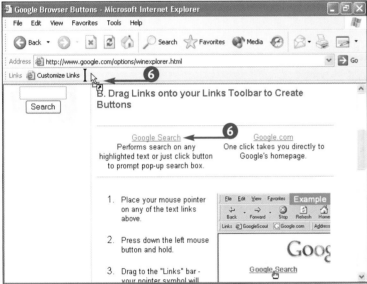

Google's Browser Buttons links appear.

⑥ Click and drag the browser button that you want up to the Links or Personal toolbar and drop it in place.

The selected button appears on your browser's toolbar.

## Attention!

When you attempt to add the Google Search button, a dialog box appears indicating that the object you are adding may be unsafe. The button is safe to add, so if you still want the button, click OK to install it.

## Desktop Trick!

You can place a shortcut icon for Google.com on your Windows desktop. Drag the Google.com link and drop it on a blank area of the desktop.

## More Options!

Many search sites, including Yahoo! and AltaVista, have their own browser toolbars. In addition, you can find and download a selection of browser toolbars at Download.com. Some of these toolbars, such as the 550 Access toolbar, enable you to search several sites with a single search entry.

# Using the
# GOOGLE SEARCH BUTTON

Tasks #31 and #32 show you how to add the Google Search and Google.com buttons to your Links or Personal toolbar. With the Google.com button, you have instant access to Google's home page. Instead of typing **www.google.com** every time that you want to search the Web, you simply click the Google.com button, and your browser opens Google's home page.

The Google Search button is even more powerful. No matter where you currently are on the Web, you can access the Google Search button to display a dialog box, in which you can enter one or more search words just as you would on Google's home page. Your browser opens Google's home page, enters the search phrase for you, and executes the search to display a list of results. And if you have a Web page opened that contains the search words you want to use, you do not even have to type the words. You can simply highlight the word(s) and start the Google search. For more about Google searches, refer to Chapter 1.

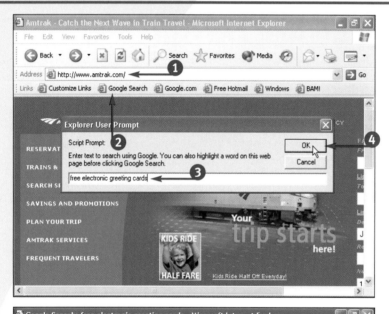

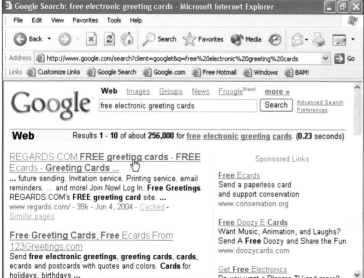

**SEARCH FROM ANY PAGE**

① Open any Web page.

② Click Google Search.

Google Search prompts you to type a search phrase.

③ Type your search phrase.

④ Click OK.

Google performs the search and displays links to any pages that contain the words you entered.

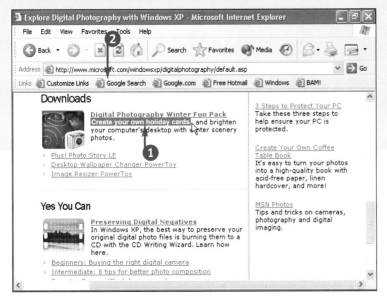

1 Select one or more
words to use as a
search phrase.

2 Click Google Search.

**# 33**

**DIFFICULTY LEVEL**

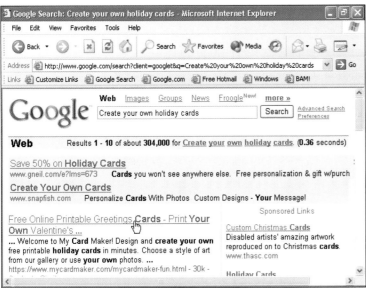

Google performs the search and displays
links to any pages that contain the words
you selected.

## Try This!
You can access Google Search with
your right mouse button. Select a
word or words on a Web page, right-
click one of the highlighted words,
and click Google Search.

## Try This!
To find pages that are similar to the
currently displayed page, right-click a
blank area of the page and click Similar
Pages. You can find pages that are
similar to a linked page by right-clicking
the link and selecting Similar Pages. Try
right-clicking various objects on a page
for additional options.

## Did You Know?
Google is constantly evolving and
may remove, rename, or add features.
Check Google regularly to stay
abreast of the latest developments.

# Install the
# GOOGLE TOOLBAR

If you use Internet Explorer as your Web browser and your computer is running Windows, you can install the Google toolbar to add it to your browser. This toolbar equips Internet Explorer with a powerful set of tools for exploring the Web and focusing Google's search results. It also provides options that allow you to vote for or against sites you visit, rank pages, highlight keywords in a document, and much more. In addition, if you are running Internet Explorer 5.5 or higher, the toolbar comes complete

with a pop-up blocker that can prevent most unsolicited Web ads from appearing in separate windows on your screen.

The Google toolbar is completely free. You download it as you would download any software, run the installation routine, and then begin using it immediately. The toolbar appears just below your other toolbars, and you can choose to hide it at any time or uninstall it if you decide that you no longer want it.

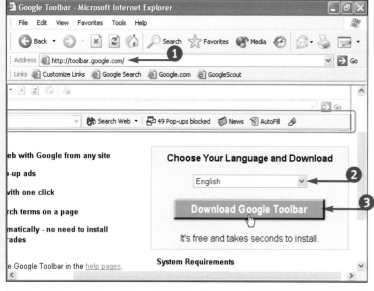

① Type **toolbar.google.com** and press Enter.

② Click here and select the language that you want.

③ Click Download Google Toolbar.

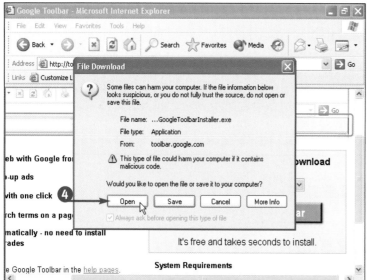

The File Download dialog box appears.

④ Click Open.

Your browser downloads the file and then automatically executes the program installation.

76

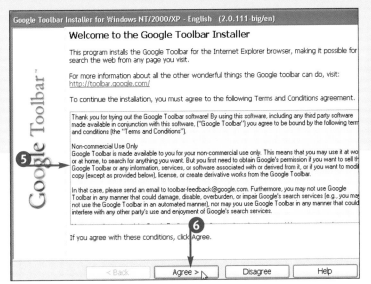

The Google Toolbar Installer program appears.

⑤ Read the license agreement.

⑥ If you agree to the terms, click Agree.

⑦ Follow the on-screen instructions to complete the installation.

**DIFFICULTY LEVEL**

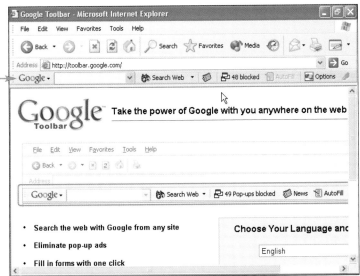

● When you run your browser, the Google toolbar appears just above the Web page viewing area.

**TIPS**

### Try This!
To hide a toolbar in Internet Explorer, including the Google toolbar, right-click the blank area of any toolbar or the menu bar and click the name of the toolbar that you want to hide. You can perform the same steps to toggle the toolbar back on.

### Remove It!
To uninstall the Google toolbar completely, click the Google button on the left end of the Google toolbar, click Help, and then click Uninstall.

### Try This!
Click the Google button on the left end of the Google toolbar and click Google Links to view links to many of Google's tools. Click Zeitgeist to check out the current list of most popular search phrases.

# SEARCH
## from the Google toolbar

The most basic task that you can perform using the Google toolbar is to search for Web pages. With this toolbar, you no longer need to go to www.google.com to perform a search. You can use the Search Web button to initiate a search at Google. This is straightforward enough, but as with most Google features, more powerful tools hide behind the simplicity of the Search Web button. As this task shows, you can search the Web not only for Web sites and specific pages but also for images, Google groups, news articles, stock quotes, and more.

In addition, the Google toolbar keeps track of the search phrases that you enter, so you can repeat the search at a later time. Have you ever performed a productive search and then wondered later just how you worded that search? The Google toolbar can help you remember. Also, if you do not want to remember or you do not want other people who use your computer to know what you searched for, you can clear the list.

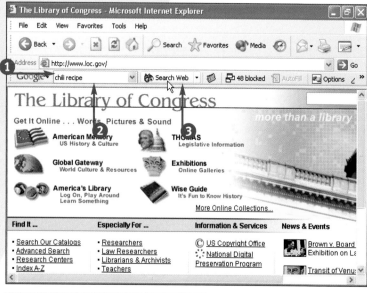

**1** Click here.

If the box already contains a search entry, Google highlights the entry.

**2** Type your search phrase.

**3** Click Search Web.

Google searches and displays links for any pages that contain the words you typed.

**4** Click here to open the Search Web drop-down list.

The Search Web drop-down list opens, displaying several alternative searches.

5 Click an option to perform a different type of search using the same search phrase.

**# 35**

**DIFFICULTY LEVEL**

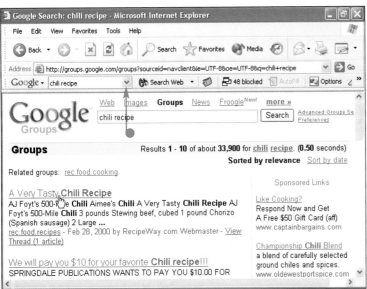

Google performs the search and displays links to any additional resources that it finds.

● You can click here to view a list of recent search phrases that you entered and click a phrase to reenter it in a search.

**TIPS**

### Did You Know?
If you enter a search phrase on Google's search page rather than in the Google toolbar's text box, the text box still records the search phrase and adds it to the list.

### Did You Know?
Google records your search phrases, and anyone who logs on to your computer can view them and know what you were searching for. To clear the list, click the Google button on the left end of the Google toolbar and click Clear Search History.

### Try This!
You can disable Google's search history option to prevent it from keeping track of your searches. See task #40 for information on how to change options.

# ALLOW POP-UPS
## at a site

Many Web sites earn money by selling advertising space or agreeing to support *pop-up ads* — windows that automatically pop up on visitors' screens. When you visit some sites, as many as half dozen pop-up ads may accost you.

Pop-up ads slow your Web browsing in two ways: They consume bandwidth and system resources that your computer uses to download the pages you really want to view, and they waste your time because you must close them. Some service providers help screen out some pop-up ads, but ads can bypass many of the systems that block them.

Now that you have the Google toolbar, you have a powerful ally to help eliminate pop-ups — Google's pop-up blocker. The pop-up blocker performs its job in the background, automatically blocking pop-ups and displaying a running count of the number of pop-ups that it successfully blocked.

However, not all pop-ups are advertisements. Some may contain useful information about a site that you want to view. This task shows you how to disable the pop-up blocker for individual sites.

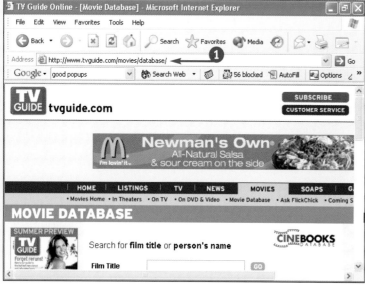

① Open a page at a site that features pop-ups you want to allow.

*Note: Google's pop-up blocker is enabled by default.*

If Google blocks a pop-up, it displays a starburst and adds to its running count of blocked pop-ups.

② Click the pop-up blocker button.

- The button's text changes to indicate that pop-ups are now allowed at this site.

③ Click your browser's Refresh button.

**DIFFICULTY LEVEL**

Your browser reloads the page and displays any pop-ups.

*Note: You can re-enable the pop-up blocker for a site at any time by returning to the site and clicking the pop-up blocker button.*

## TIPS

### Try This!
To bypass the pop-up blocker without disabling it for a site, hold down the Ctrl key while opening or refreshing the page. To reset the pop-up counter, hold down the Shift and Alt keys while clicking the pop-up blocker button.

### Important!
If you enable the pop-up blocker and still receive pop-ups, adware is probably installed on your computer. To find and remove adware, you need to install and run a spyware/adware removal utility such as Ad-Aware or Spybot Search & Destroy. You can find such utilities at www.download.com.

### Did You Know?
When you click the pop-up blocker button to allow pop-ups at a particular site, the pop-up blocker adds the site to a *whitelist* of sites where pop-ups are allowed.

# Search for
# INFORMATION ON A PAGE

Web pages often contain much more information than you really need, burying the specific information that you want under a mound of text. You can use your browser's Find feature on the Edit menu to search for specific words or phrases on a page, but that requires several time-consuming steps. And if the page contains multiple occurrences of the search word or phrase, you must skip from one occurrence to the next to determine if the selection contains the information that you want.

The Google toolbar offers a better alternative — a highlighter that marks the occurrence of each search word on a page. You can use the highlighter whenever you want to search for specific words or phrases on a page. After you perform a Google search and open one of the pages listed in Google's search results, you can activate the highlighter to have Google highlight the occurrences of words that are in your search phrase. Or you can enter a new set of words in the toolbar's Search text box and activate the highlighter to have Google highlight any occurrences of those words.

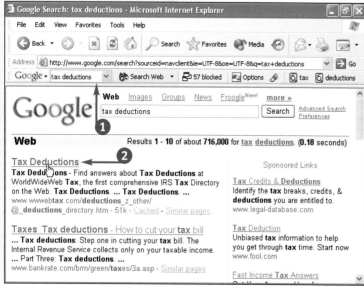

① Perform a search using the Google toolbar.

*Note: See task #35 for more information.*

② Click a link to open one of the pages in Google's search results.

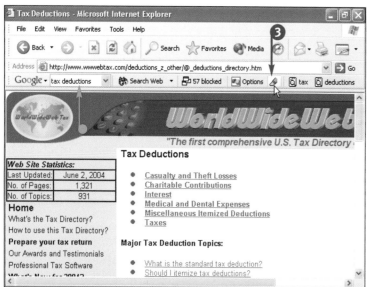

Your browser opens and displays the selected Web page.

● The search phrase remains in the Search box.

③ Click the Highlight button.

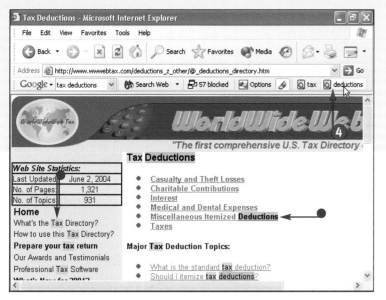

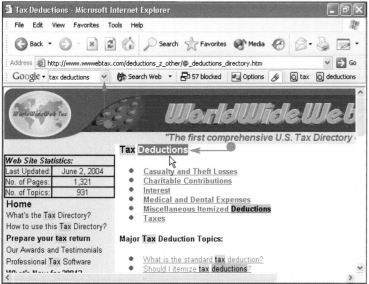

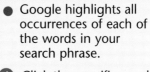

- Google highlights all occurrences of each of the words in your search phrase.

④ Click the specific word that you want to find.

# 37

**DIFFICULTY LEVEL**

- Google jumps to the first occurrence of the word.

- You can continue to click the word to jump ahead to each subsequent occurrence of the word.

**TIPS**

### Did You Know?

Even if you do not use a Google search to find and open a page, you can use the highlighter (🖉) to mark words on the page. With the page displayed, type the word or words that you want to highlight. Resist the temptation to press the Enter key. Click the Highlight button.

### Remove It!

The Highlight button toggles highlighting on and off. To remove highlighting, simply click the Highlight button again.

### Try This!

When you enter two or more words in a search phrase, Google highlights each search word in a different color. To have Google treat your entire search phrase as a single entry, enclose the phrase in quotation marks.

# Streamline online forms with
# AUTOFILL

Many Web sites contain forms that enable you to register for services or free offers, order products or services, or provide feedback. Entering your name, address, e-mail address, and other information into these forms can be time-consuming, especially if you complete forms fairly often.

Fortunately, Google can automate the process for the most common types of data entries: your name, mailing address, e-mail address, phone number, and credit card information. You enter this information

once in Google, and Google stores it in an encrypted format to keep it private.

When you visit a site that contains a form, Google checks the text boxes to determine if it has any information that it can fill in for you. If Google has a data entry that matches the type of entry required by one of the text boxes, it highlights the box yellow and activates AutoFill. Assuming that you trust the site enough to enter information, you can click AutoFill to have it fill in any of the highlighted text boxes.

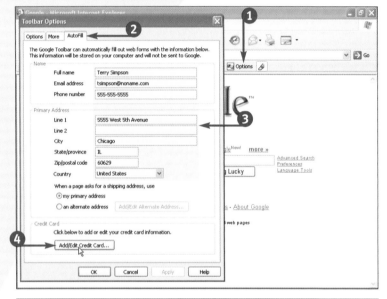

84

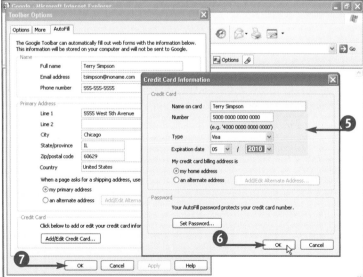

### ENTER AUTOFILL DATA

① Click Options.

The Toolbar Options dialog box appears.

② Click the AutoFill tab.

③ Type any personal information that you want Google to use to fill out forms.

④ Click Add/Edit Credit Card.

The Credit Card Information dialog box appears.

⑤ Type any credit card information that you want Google to use to fill out forms.

⑥ Click OK.

AutoFill saves your credit card information and returns you to the Toolbar Options dialog box.

⑦ Click OK.

AutoFill saves your personal information.

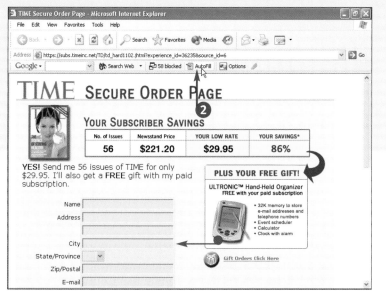

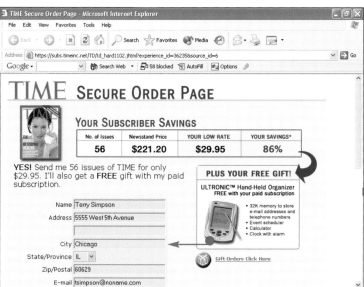

① Open a Web page that has boxes calling for information that matches the type of information you entered in AutoFill.

The AutoFill button becomes active.

DIFFICULTY LEVEL

● AutoFill highlights any boxes that it can fill in.

② Click AutoFill.

● AutoFill completes as much of the form as possible and prompts you for confirmation to enter credit card information, if the form calls for it.

## Try This!

When you click the AutoFill button, AutoFill automatically fills in as many empty form boxes that it has information for. To see which data entries AutoFill is about to fill in, hold down the Shift key while clicking the AutoFill button. AutoFill displays the Confirm AutoFill dialog box, showing you the information it is about to enter. Click OK to enter the information or Cancel to abort the operation.

## Did You Know?

You need not type entries into all blanks on the AutoFill tab in the Toolbar Options dialog box. However, if you click the AutoFill button when one of its blanks does not contain an entry requested on the form, AutoFill prompts you to enter the information so that it can enter it for you.

# CUSTOMIZE
## the Google toolbar

Although the Google toolbar is quite powerful in its default condition, you can overhaul its operation. You can disable the search history list or pop-up blocker, select the Google search site that you want Google to use when it searches, have search results displayed in a new window, and much more. You do all this by displaying and using the Toolbar Options dialog box, as shown in this task.

By default, most of the options in the Toolbar Options dialog box are enabled. Two options not enabled by default are PageRank and Page Info Menu. The

PageRank indicator displays the relative importance of the page you are viewing according to an automatic calculation that Google performs. You can use the Page Info Menu option to view a cached snapshot of the page, display links to similar pages, show backward links — which are pages that link to this page — or translate the page into English.

In this task, you learn how to make some very basic changes to the Google toolbar by enabling or disabling some of its features and components.

① Click Options.

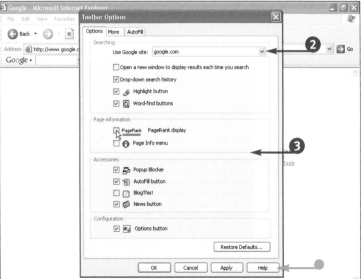

The Toolbar Options dialog box appears, displaying the Options tab.

② Click here and select the search site for the country in which you want to search.

③ Click any option on or off.

● You can click Help for additional information about the options.

4 Click OK.

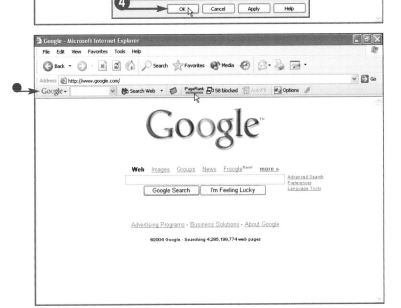

● The Google toolbar's appearance reflects any toolbar options that you changed.

TIPS

### Did You Know?

If you realize that you do not like the changes you made to the toolbar, you can click the Restore Defaults button at the bottom of the Toolbar Options dialog box to return the toolbar to its original condition.

### Important!

With PageRank enabled, the toolbar automatically forwards the URL of any Web page that you visit to Google to help it determine page rankings. For more information, click the Google button, click Help, and then click Privacy Information.

### More Options!

The Google toolbar is like any other toolbar in your browser; you can drag the Google toolbar's left end up or down to place the toolbar on another line, or you can drag it left or right to resize it. You can right-click a blank area of any toolbar and click Google to toggle the toolbar on or off.

# Check and change
# ADVANCED OPTIONS

The Toolbar Options dialog box has an Options tab that enables you to customize the toolbar by changing several settings. But those options are a small sampling of what the dialog box has to offer. On the More tab, you can enter settings that control the way Google searches and the way you navigate found sites. You can also turn on buttons for performing special searches, such as searching for images and discussion groups.

The More tab's offerings go beyond what a short task can cover, but a few options are notable, especially

those in the Web Buttons group. The Up button takes you up one level in the URL's directory tree. If you are viewing www.website.com/directory/subdirectory, clicking the Up button opens www.website.com/directory/. The Next and Previous buttons enable you to flip through a list of pages from Google's search results without having to return to Google's search results. The Category button displays the Google Directory. And you can use the Voting buttons to give a site a positive or negative vote.

❶ Click Options.

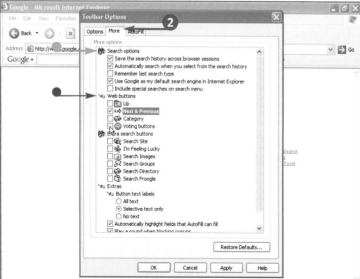

The Toolbar Options dialog box appears.

❷ Click the More tab.

❸ Click any option on or off.

● The Search Options give you control over how Google performs searches.

● The Web Buttons options provide tools for navigating and ranking Web sites.

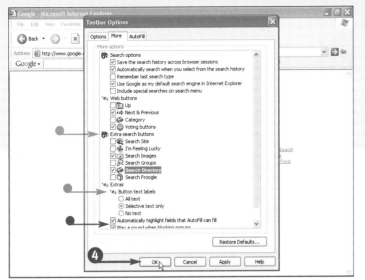

- The Extra Search Buttons options enable you to turn on special search buttons for Google Groups, Images, and Froogle and other Google features.

**DIFFICULTY LEVEL**

- The Button Text Labels options control the amount of text that describes each button.

- Additional options give you control over AutoFill, sounds, and the pop-up blocker count.

④ Click OK.

- The Google toolbar's appearance reflects any toolbar options that you changed.

## TIPS

### Did You Know?
The buttons listed under Extra Search Buttons behave differently depending on whether you type text in the Search box before clicking the button. If the Search box contains an entry, the button initiates a search using that entry. If the box is blank, the button takes you to the Google search site where you can perform the search.

### Did You Know?
If you add a check mark to the Include Special Searches on Search Menu option (☐ changes to ☑), Google tacks a list of special searches to the end of the Search Web menu. These include options to search Microsoft, Apple Macintosh, and U.S. Government sites.

### Try This!
For more information about the options on the More tab, click the Help button at the bottom of the Toolbar Options dialog box.

# Get Your News through Google News

Many users have their favorite news sites, including CNN.com, FOXNews.com, ABC News, and CBSNews.com, but few of these sites feature the global coverage and breadth that Google offers. At Google News, you can access headlines, photos, and reports extracted from approximately 4,500 news sources around the world. This provides you with several perspectives of the same event or topic and often introduces you to stories that the major media outlets do not carry.

Google constantly updates its headline page throughout the day, so every time that you visit, you receive up-to-the-minute reports. In addition, Google automatically arranges the stories to present the most significant and relevant information first. You can click the link that accompanies a headline to go directly to the Web site of the featured news source or

click a link that follows the report summary to find out what other sources report about the same incident.

Google News features a navigation bar that you can use to access world and national news, business news, science and technology reports, sports scores and features, entertainment news, and articles about health and fitness.

For your convenience, Google provides a link that you can click to make Google News your browser's home page. You can also register for news alerts to have Google e-mail you when it finds an article that matches your interests. This chapter shows you how to take full advantage of Google News. At the writing of this book, Google News features were still in the Beta testing phase and many screens display "Beta."

# Top 100

# GOOGLE NEWS

When you open the Google News home page, it features a collection of the top headlines from around the world. Using the navigation bar on the left, you can quickly jump to a specific section: World, U.S., Business, Sci/Tech, Sports, Entertainment, or Health.

The center column features the current top headlines along with the first 25 words or so of each featured article. Each headline is a link you can click to jump to the Web site of the source for the full story. Google also offers a link that you can click to view a list of other sources carrying the same story, as task #43 demonstrates.

The column on the right contains a list of stories from the sections other than Top Stories. Usually, Google provides a link to the top story in sports, science and technology, business, entertainment, and health. This column also provides a list of hot topics — politicians, celebrities, or places in the news. You can scroll down the page for additional stories or scroll to the bottom to check out links to Google's international news for other countries.

① Type **news.google.com** and press Enter.

Your browser displays the Google News home page.

② Click the story's headline.

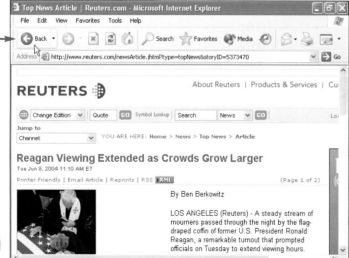

Your browser opens the source, where you can read the original article.

③ Click Back.

Your browser returns to the Google News home page.

● Google displays a link to the top story in each news category.

④ Click the link in the navigation bar for the news category that you want.

DIFFICULTY LEVEL

Google displays a list of links to reports in the selected category.

## Try This!
Google's home page contains a link to Google News. Go to the home page at www.google.com and click the News link. If you installed the Google toolbar (see task #34), you can click the Google News button (🗐) for instant access to Google News.

## Try This!
Right-click the link for a story that you want to read and click Open in New Window to display it in a separate window. You can then close the window to quickly return to Google's headlines.

## Try This!
If the Google News home page has been open for several minutes, click your browser's Refresh button (🗐) to refresh the page with any updated headlines.

# SORT STORIES
## by date

When Google displays a list of links to various sources that cover a story, it lists the most relevant stories first. How Google determines relevance is a company secret. Google uses several criteria, including how many other pages link to a particular page to determine the relative importance of the information. The rankings are automated, so just because an article lands at the top of the list, Google does not guarantee that this is the most insightful or current article in its news index.

Google does offer another way to sort the articles. You can choose to sort the articles by date instead of by relevance. Google arranges the articles chronologically, listing links to the most recent articles first. The sort option also enables you to follow a current event back in time to gain a historical perspective of a particular issue or event.

You can always return to the listing that Google sorts by relevance by clicking the Sort by Relevance link, as shown in this task.

❶ Type **news.google.com** and press Enter.

❷ Click the link for displaying sources related to the featured article.

Google displays a list of articles sorted by relevance.

❸ Click Sort by Date.

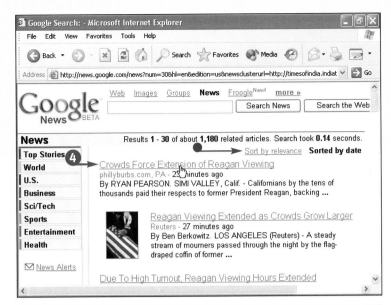

Google sorts the list of articles by date and time, displaying the most current article first.

● You can click Sort by Relevance to return to the relevance listing.

④ Click the link for the most current article.

Your browser opens the article from the source and displays it.

## TIPS

### Did You Know?

The article that Google lists as the most current is only the article Google has most recently added to its index. It may not be the most current. In addition, if a particular source was late in reporting the story, its story may be listed first, even though the source was not the first to report the story.

### Did You Know?

The Sort by Date option is available for all sections of Google News and is especially useful when accessing late-breaking sports news.

### More Options

If you are following a story closely, consider signing up for Google news alerts, as shown in task #49. Google can help you keep track of late-breaking reports via e-mail.

# Explore multiple
# NEWS SOURCES

You can use Google News as a standard news and information service to scan headlines and read stories, but Google News provides much more depth of coverage. Google follows nearly every news story with a link to other sources that cover the same story. When you click the link for viewing related sources, Google typically displays a list of links and report summaries to dozens, and sometimes hundreds, of other sites. Many of these sites receive the story from the same news organization, such as the AP news service, but other sites often have their own reporters at the scene and provide additional information that you can obtain nowhere else. By digging through stories at these other sites, you can gain a fuller understanding of a particular incident or event.

Because Google News automatically gathers, sorts, and groups reports from nearly 4,500 news organizations, you can expect to receive some results that do not quite fit the group, but the grouping is fairly accurate.

❶ Type **news.google.com** and press Enter.

❷ Click the news category that you want.

Google displays headlines and summaries for stories in the selected category.

❸ Scroll down to the summary of a story that you want to explore.

❹ Click the Related link that follows the story summary.

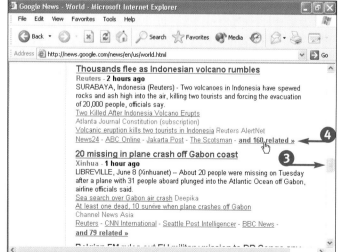

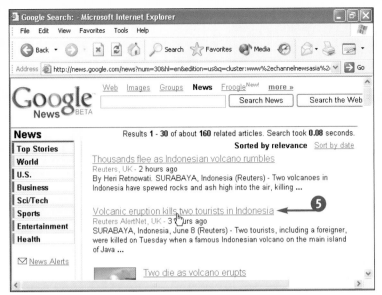

- Google News displays headlines and summaries from related sources.

⑤ Click the link for the story that you want to read.

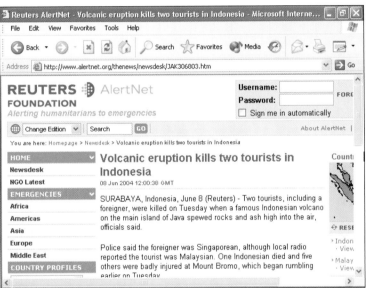

Your browser opens the story from its original source and displays it.

## TIPS

### Did You Know?

Google welcomes feedback about its news feature, so if you are not satisfied with the results or you have suggestions for improving the feature, send feedback to news-feedback@ google.com.

### Did You Know?

Google employs a special algorithm that uses several criteria to determine the relevance of an article. Google measures relevancy based in large part on the number of news sites that cover the story and how these sites position the story. However, Google's algorithm can return articles that are not covered by the mainstream media, as well.

### Try This!

Display the Google News home page and scroll down to the In the News section on the right side of the page. Click the link for a celebrity, politician, or place, and then click the headline to read the entire story.

# Search for a
# SPECIFIC NEWS STORY

Google News delivers up-to-the-minute headline news right to your browser. However, the stories considered headline-worthy to news organizations and to Google News may not be the most relevant to you. Maybe you are following the career of a favorite public figure or are interested in the latest news about global warming. In such cases, you can search Google News for specific articles by topic.

Google's News feature coupled with its powerful search tools places the news and information that interests you right at your fingertips. When you

search for a person, place, or topic of interest, Google News performs your search and delivers a list of links to related stories. If several news organizations report the same or similar stories, Google provides a link that you can click to check out those other sources, as well.

As with Google's Web search, Google drops any common words from your search phrase, so when you type a search phrase, focus on descriptive words.

① Type **news.google.com** and press Enter.

Google News displays the headline news.

② Click here and type one or more words describing your interest.

③ Click Search News.

Google displays a selection of news articles that contain your search word(s).

● You can click Sort by Date to list the articles in chronological order with the most recent article first.

④ Click the link for the article that you want to read.

Your browser displays the original article at the source Web site.

## TIPS

### Try This!

For a more focused search, search for an exact phrase by enclosing it in quotation marks. This is the same technique that you use to focus a Google Web search, as shown in task #6.

### Did You Know?

You may expect that when you are in a specific news section, a search from that section would turn up news related only to that section. However, when you perform a search from any area of Google News, Google searches the entire news index.

### More Options!

If you installed the Google toolbar in task #34, you can search Google news from the toolbar. Type your search words in the Search box, click the ▾ to the right of the Search Web button, and choose Search News.

# ADVANCED NEWS SEARCH

You may not see the Advanced News Search option on the Google News opening page, but after you perform a basic search for news articles, the option appears to the right of the Search buttons. The Advanced News Search feature provides additional options for broadening or narrowing your search. For example, you can type your search words in the Find Results with at Least One of the Words box to have Google find articles that contain any one of the words in your search phrase.

Using an advanced news search, you can narrow your search to a specific news organization, such as CNN or *USA Today* or limit the results to news organizations in a particular country or U.S. state. You can focus your search by having Google return only those articles that have your search words in the headline or in the URL of the article. You can also specify a range of dates to limit your search to a particular time period.

1 Type **news.google.com** and press Enter.

2 Click here and type one or more words that describe your interest.

3 Click Search News.

Google displays a list of articles that contain all the words you entered.

4 Click Advanced News Search.

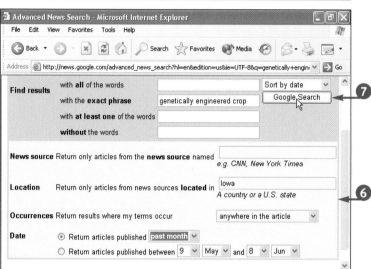

# 45

**DIFFICULTY LEVEL**

Google's Advanced News Search form appears, with your search phrase in this box.

● You can highlight and drag your search term to another Find Results box.

**⑤** Click here and select your sort preference.

**⑥** Enter any additional search preferences.

**⑦** Click Google Search.

If Google finds any articles that match your search instructions, it displays their headlines, which you can click to access the sources.

**TIPS**

## Did You Know?

Google News provides access to stories reported in the past 30 days. Searching for older stories may return few results. You may have better luck by performing a Google Web search to find articles that other sites have archived.

## Try This!

You can perform an advanced search without using the Advanced News Search form. Use Boolean operators, such as OR and – (NOT) to construct your search phrase. You can use special Google search operators as well. You can use the Google News **source:** operator to limit your search to a specific news organization — for example, type **middle east peace source:new_york_times**. Use the **location:** operator to limit your search to news organizations in a specific country or U.S. state.

# Select your
# NATIONAL INTEREST

Google News is truly cosmopolitan, enabling you to access Google News for at least ten different countries: Australia, Canada, France, Germany, India, Italy, New Zealand, Spain, the United Kingdom, and the United States. Also, Google News delivers news in at least five different languages: English, French, German, Italian, and Spanish. By the time you read this, Google News may feature expanded coverage.

Selecting a national interest still provides access to international — or world — news, but when you choose to browse national news, Google serves up stories from news organizations in the selected country. In addition, the links for Business, Sci/Tech, Sports, Entertainment, and Health rank stories of national interest first, followed by stories from news organizations located in other countries.

No matter which national interest you select, Google provides you with links to stories from news organizations all around the world. However, by selecting a different national interest, you can often gain a better global perspective. You can also obtain a clearer sense of how various news organizations slant their reports.

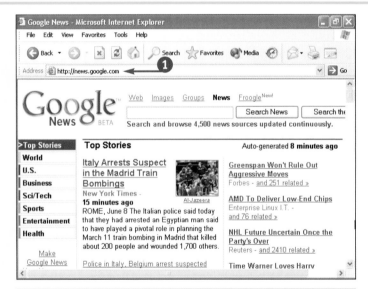

**①** Type **news.google.com** and press Enter.

Google News displays the latest headline news.

**②** Scroll down the page.

**③** Click a link to specify the national interest that you want.

Google News displays the relevant headline news for the country that you selected.

④ Click the link to view the selected country's national news.

Google displays summaries of and links to the current top stories in the selected country.

## TIPS

### Did You Know?

When you search Google News, it returns links to stories from news organizations all over the world, even though you are at a Google News site for a particular country. To limit your search to stories from news organizations within a specific country, perform an advanced search, as shown in task #45.

### Try This!

Click the link for your home country, search for a topic of interest, and make a mental note of the headline stories that Google returns. Then click the link for a different country and perform the same search. You may find more similarities than differences, especially if you search two English-language sites. Now perform the same search with the addition of the location: operator followed by the country name. The search results are now limited to sources from the specified country.

# TRANSLATE STORIES
## from the foreign press

Because Google News delivers reports from news organizations all around the world, you have a fairly good chance of encountering articles in a foreign language. If you access Google News in a country where news sources report in a language other than your native tongue, you will almost assuredly encounter articles in a foreign language.

Although this does present an obstacle for accessing the news from foreign countries, the obstacle is not insurmountable. Google's translator can translate

nearly any article into the most common languages. If you are an English speaker, for example, and you encounter an article written in French, Google's translator can translate the article into English so that you can read it.

As explained in task #28, Google's translator is an automated translation tool that can provide you with a rudimentary translation. The translation can be quite rough, but it usually provides you with a general understanding of an article.

**①** Type **news.google.com** and press Enter.

Google News displays the current top stories.

**②** Scroll down the page.

**③** Click a link to a country that presents news in a foreign language.

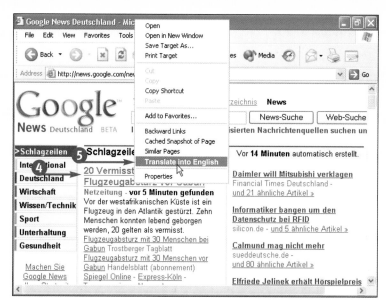

Google News displays the relevant headline news for the country that you selected.

④ Right-click the link to a story you want to read that is in the foreign language.

⑤ Click Translate into *X*, where *X* is your language.

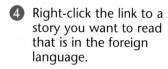

**DIFFICULTY LEVEL**

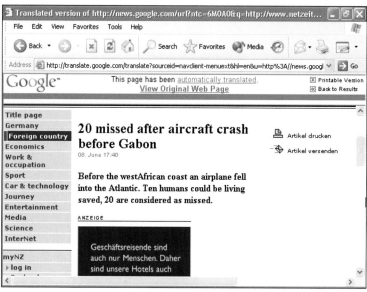

Google displays a message indicating that it is translating the page, and then it displays the page in the selected language.

## TIPS

### Try This!

If the article in the foreign language is already displayed, right-click a blank area of the page, and click the Translate into *X* option, where *X* is your language.

### Did You Know?

Google options appear in the primary language of the country that you selected. If you go to Google Italia, for example, the Search News button appears as the Cerca nelle news button. When you translate the page, Google does not translate the button names.

### More Options!

Google features many more language options on its Preferences page. Chapter 1 shows how to enter your preferences in Google.

# Make Google News your
# BROWSER'S HOME PAGE

Most people who browse the Web have a favorite site that they gravitate toward whenever they start their browsers. If you typically perform a search immediately after starting your browser, you can set up your browser to open Google's home page, or if you access your e-mail via the Web, you can set up your browser to open the site where you check for mail. Many people like to scan the news headlines first thing to see if any significant events have occurred lately.

You can specify a home page in most browsers by displaying the Preferences or Internet Options dialog box and entering the URL for the page you want to use. Or you can open the page, display the Preferences or Internet Options dialog box, and then click an option for using the current page as the browser's home page.

Google News makes setting the home page even easier. If you want to use Google News as your browser's home page, you simply click a link, as shown in this task.

① Type **news.google.com** and press Enter.

Google News displays the current top stories.

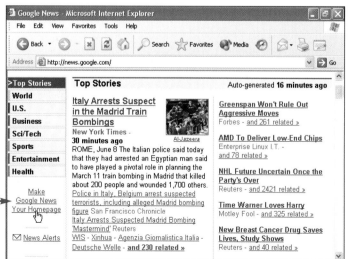

② Click Make Google News Your Homepage.

## 48

DIFFICULTY LEVEL

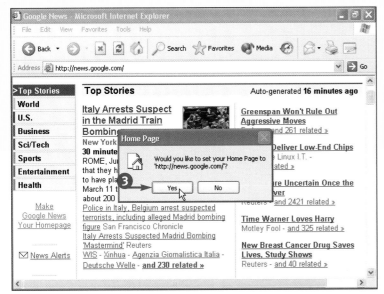

The Home Page dialog box appears, prompting you to confirm that you want to set Google News as your home page.

**③** Click Yes.

Google News sets itself up as your browser's home page.

● Whenever you start your browser, it automatically loads Google News.

---

**TIPS**

### Remove It!

You can change your Web browser's home page back at any time. In Internet Explorer, open the page that you want to use, click Tools, Internet Options, Use Current, and then OK. In Netscape Navigator, open the page that you want to use, click Edit, Preferences, Use Current Page, and then click OK.

### Try This!

If you installed the Google toolbar in task #34, you have quick access to Google News without having to reset your home page. Click the Google button, Google Links, and then Google News, or simply click the Google News button (▨).

### Desktop Trick!

Create a shortcut to Google News on your Windows desktop. Click a blank area of the Google News page, Create Shortcut, and then OK.

---

# ALERTS VIA E-MAIL

Why spend time checking the news when you can have Google keep you posted concerning any late-breaking developments? By registering for news alerts, you can have Google notify you, via e-mail, whenever it discovers an article that includes the words in your search phrase. Each e-mail message contains the first few lines of one or more articles along with a link for each article that you can click to connect to the source Web site for the story.

Requesting a Google news alert is fairly simple. You need only enter your search phrase and e-mail

address and specify how often you want Google to alert you — as the story breaks or once a day. Before Google can notify you, it must confirm your e-mail address. Google does this by sending you a confirmation message that you must reply to by clicking a link in the message. This prevents users from sending news alerts to other users.

After Google receives your confirmation, Google begins monitoring the news for you and informing you of any breaking news.

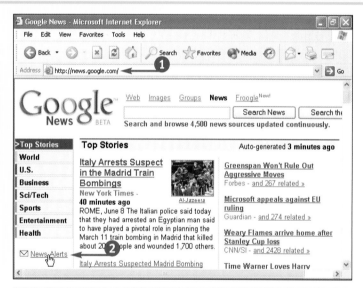

① Type **news.google.com** and press Enter.

② Click News Alerts.

The Google News Alerts page appears.

③ Click here and type words that describe your topic of interest.

④ Click here and select how often you want to receive alerts.

⑤ Click here and type your e-mail address.

⑥ Click Create News Alert.

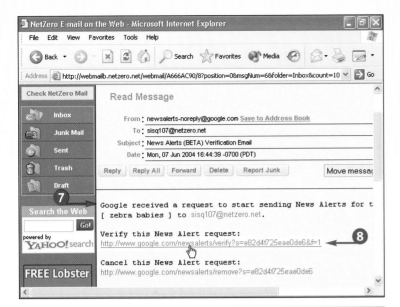

## 49

Google displays a message indicating that you must confirm your e-mail address.

⑦ Check your e-mail account and display the confirmation message.

⑧ Click the link in the message to confirm your e-mail address.

Google begins monitoring the news for you.

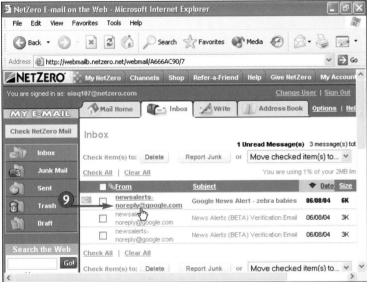

When Google discovers an article that contains your search words, it e-mails the article to you.

⑨ Click the link for reading the article.

The link connects you to Google, where you can read the article.

# TIPS

## Remove It!
Every news alert e-mail message you receive from Google contains a link you can click to cancel the alert.

## Did You Know?
You cannot edit a news alert. However, you can easily cancel a news alert and create a new alert with the search phrase that you want to use.

## Try This!
To incorporate advanced search operators into your search, perform an advanced search as shown in task #45. Highlight the search phrase in Google's Search text box, which contains the search phrase complete with advanced search operators. Press Ctrl+C to copy it. Go to the Google News Alerts page and paste the search phrase into the News Search text box.

# Get news
# ABOUT GOOGLE

Because Google is so busy gathering news from around the world, few users realize that Google itself is a newsworthy item. Google is constantly evolving and offering new, more powerful tools for navigating and managing Internet resources. To keep abreast of the latest developments, you can "google" Google. Simply go to Google's search page at www.google.com, type **google**, press Enter, and follow the trail of links to various news stories about Google. You may be surprised at just how much of a celebrity Google is.

However, googling Google also turns up a fair share of articles that are highly, and often unjustifiably, critical of Google and its business practices. Approach these articles as you approach most reporting on the Internet — with a healthy dose of skepticism.

You can obtain official reports and press releases from Google itself by visiting Google's Press area. This task shows you two sources where you can obtain reliable information about Google, including Google's About page and Google Help Central, where you can learn about Google's latest additions.

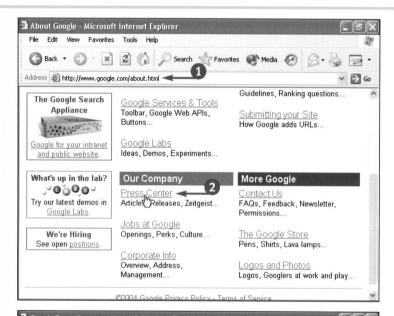

### ACCESS THE GOOGLE PRESS CENTER

1 Type **www.google.com/ about.html** and press Enter.

The About Google page appears, displaying links to several areas where you can obtain information.

2 Click Press Center.

Google displays links to various newsworthy items, including company information and new features.

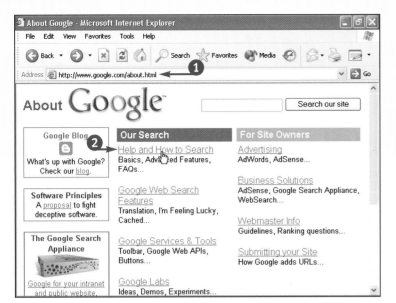

**DIFFICULTY LEVEL**

1. Type **www.google.com/about.html** and press Enter.

   The About Google page appears, displaying links to several areas where you can obtain information.

2. Click Help and How to Search.

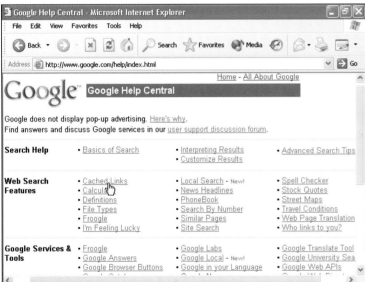

Google Help Central appears, displaying links to Google's many features.

*Note: Visit Google Help Central regularly to learn about new Google features.*

---

## TIPS

### More Options!
Google Groups has its own discussion forum in which Google users help each other learn and use its many features. Chapter 8 explores Google groups. To access this discussion forum, click the User Support Discussion Forum link near the top of Google Help Central.

### Did You Know?
This book focuses on making full use of Google's many features, but if you are a Web page author or are trying to promote your business through Google, you can find a great deal of helpful information. Go to the About Google page and check out the links under For Site Owners.

### Check It Out!
You can obtain unbiased news about Google at www.watchinggooglelike ahawk.com. This site contains links to news stories about Google, popular new features, and Google tips.

# Explore the Local Scene with Google

Google serves as your portal to the global offerings of the Web, but Google can guide you through your own city, town, or neighborhood, too. Google combines its index of more than 4 billion Web pages with *Yellow Pages* information to create a powerful geographical search tool that it calls Google Local. With Google Local, you can focus your search on a specific area or region in the United States to find restaurants, hotels, auto repair shops, museums, government offices, and other places of interest within a specified radius.

With Google Local, you can pitch your *Yellow Pages* phone books and city maps in the trash. You simply enter your address and zip code, and Google Local stores it for you. When you need to find a particular business or organization, you enter a word or two to

describe what you are looking for and then click a button to send Google on a search. Almost immediately, Google returns a list of links to the closest places that may carry the product or offer the services you need. You simply click a link to obtain the phone number or address or to go to an online map service, such as MapQuest, to obtain driving directions.

This chapter shows you how to use Google as your personal neighborhood tour guide and information kiosk. You learn how to connect to Google Local, perform a search, narrow or broaden your search, and obtain driving directions. If you are a business owner and would like to have your business included in Google's search results, this chapter shows you just what to do.

# Top 100

# PERFORM A LOCAL SEARCH
## from Google's home page

Google is much smarter than most users realize. When you enter a search phrase, Google not only looks for Web pages that contain all the words in your search phrase, but it also analyzes the phrase for any character strings that suggest a special search. Knowing the types of character strings that trigger a special search, you can add these strings to your search phrase to perform a local search. For example, you can add your zip code or city name to your search phrase to have Google include local search results in its list of links.

Most entries that Google returns contain the name of the business or organization, its address, and its phone number. You can click the link for a business or organization to view a map showing its location. You can then click another link to go directly to an online map service to obtain directions.

Performing a local search from Google's home page does not provide access to all the features that Google Local has to offer, but it does provide a quick and easy search that can steer you in the right direction.

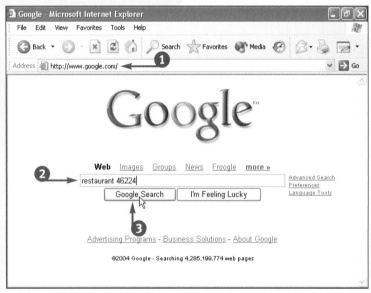

① Type **www.google.com** and press Enter.

② Type your search phrase, including a zip code or city name of the area that you want to search.

③ Click Google Search.

Google displays a list of search results, with any Google Local results at the top.

④ Click the Local Results link.

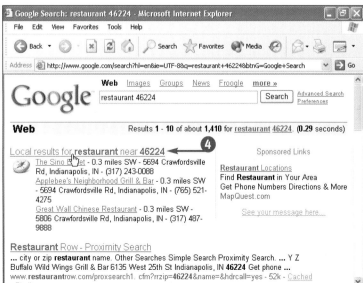

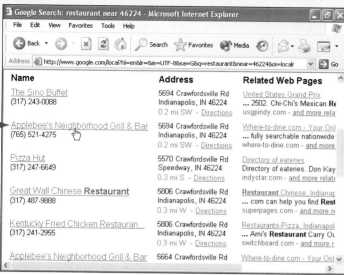

Google displays a longer list of businesses or organizations that match your search phrase.

⑤ Click the link for one of the businesses or organizations.

**# 51**

DIFFICULTY LEVEL

Google displays a map showing the location of the selected business or organization.

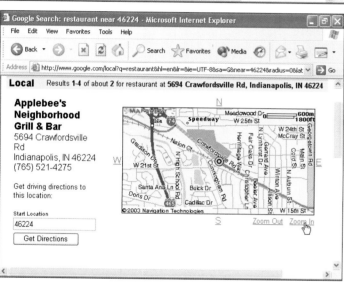

## Try This!

When the map appears, click Zoom In to zoom in on the map and obtain a clearer idea of where the selected business or organization is located. Refer to tasks #56 and #57 for more information about maps and directions.

## Did You Know?

Because Google Local relies on Web data to generate listings, smaller businesses and organizations that do not have their own Web sites may not appear in the search results. If you search for Italian restaurants in your area, for example, chain restaurants, such as Olive Garden, are more likely to appear than smaller establishments that do not have a strong Web presence.

# Access
# GOOGLE LOCAL

You can perform a Google local search from Google's home page, as shown in task #51, but Google features a Google Local page that provides a more robust interface for performing local searches. Google Local provides two search boxes — one for your search phrase and the other for your address.

In addition to enabling you to perform local searches, Google Local offers the option of saving your address for future searches. If you choose to save your address, you never need to enter it again to perform

a local search. You can simply go to Google Local, type one or two words to describe the product or service that you want, and click the Google Search button.

If you choose to have Google Local save your address, it does not affect searches you perform from Google's home page. For example, if you search for "auto parts" from Google's home page, you still need to add a zip code or city name to trigger a local search.

① Type **www.google.com** and press Enter.

② Click More.

Google's More, More, More page appears.

③ Click Google Local.

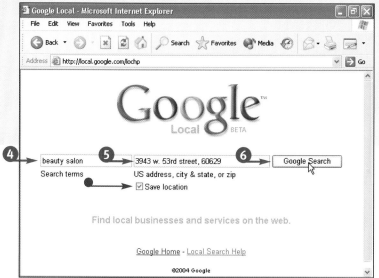

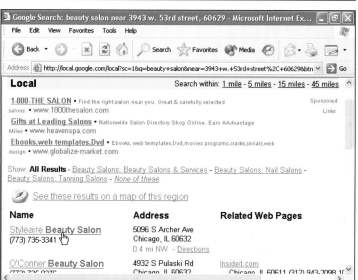

Google Local appears.

**Note:** *At the writing of this book, Google Local was still in the Beta testing phase, so "Beta" appears in these figures.*

④ Type one or more words to describe the product or service that you want.

⑤ Type your street address, followed by your city and state or your zip code.

● You can click here to have Google Local save your address.

⑥ Click Google Search.

Google Local displays a list of businesses or organizations that offer the specified product or service.

## Try This!

Does your local police station or fire department have a Web site? If so, Google Local may be able to provide its location and phone number. Try searching Google Local for **police**, **fire department**, or **government** and see what turns up.

## Try This!

Instead of accessing Google Local from Google's home page, go there directly. Type **local.google.com** in your browser's address bar and press Enter.

## Did You Know?

During the writing of this book, Google Local did not fully support Google's SafeSearch filtering, but developers were working on it. By the time you read this book, you may be able to filter the results.

# REFINE
## your search

Google and Boolean operators have little effect in Google local searches, and Google Local does not provide an advanced search page, so trying to refine your search with special characters is usually futile. However, you can refine your search in other ways. You can click links in the search results, as shown in this task, to search various category listings or revise your search phrase. Task #54 shows how to broaden and narrow your search geographically by expanding or contracting the radius of the search by a specified number of miles.

When you perform a local search, examine the search results carefully. Google usually displays several links that you can click to take your search in a different direction. This task takes you on a tour of the search results page to show you where to look. In addition, Google always displays your original search phrase above and below the search results, so you can edit your search phrase and execute a new search.

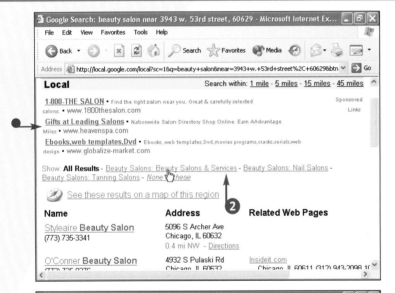

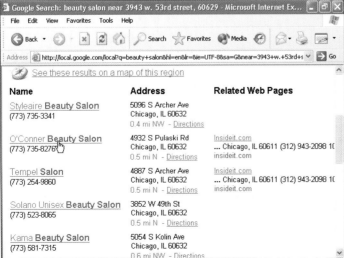

## SEARCH BY CATEGORY

① Perform a Google local search as you normally would.

This example uses "beauty salon" as the search term.

Google Local displays its search results.

● You can click a sponsor link to shop online.

② Click the link for a category related to the search results.

Google displays phone book listings for businesses or organizations in the selected category.

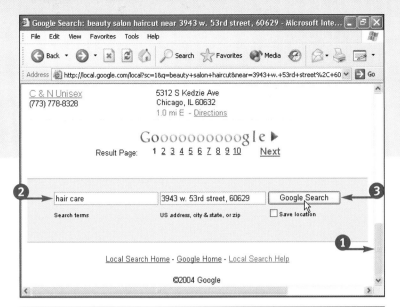

Google displays new search results based on your refined search phrase.

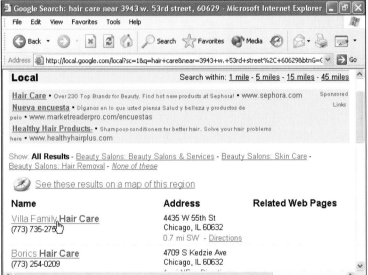

## TIPS

### Try This!
Be creative and flexible when you search. If Google Local returns search results that do not include useful entries, rephrase your search, follow the phone book categories, or click one of the related pages links to follow a different path, as shown in task #55.

### Did You Know?
Just above the list of search results, Google Local displays phone book categories included in the search. If these phone book categories have nothing to do with the product or service that you are looking for, click the None of These link that follows the list of categories. Google searches again, excluding any items from these categories.

### Try This!
Examine the search results to discover keywords that are more descriptive. Use these descriptive keywords to refine your search.

# BROADEN OR NARROW
## your search geographically

When you perform a local search, Google Local does its best to find businesses and organizations that are near the location you specify. If Google returns no search results, you can try to expand the search area or enter more general search terms to broaden your search. If Google returns search results pointing to businesses or organizations beyond the distance that you are willing to travel, you can limit the search to a smaller geographical area or enter a more specific search phrase.

As you search, you may notice that Google does not always display the closest businesses and

organizations first. Google sorts the list based not only on distance but also relevance — how likely it is that a particular business or organization offers the product or service you need. An effective search balances distance and relevance to help you find the product or service that you need as close by as possible.

If Google still does not locate any matching businesses or organizations, try shopping online at Froogle, as shown in Chapter 7.

① Type **local.google.com** and press Enter.

② Type a description of the product or service that you want.

③ Type an entry to specify the geographical area that you want to search.

*Note: If Google has saved your address, you can skip step 3.*

④ Click Google Search.

If Google finds any businesses that offer the product or service you described, it displays them.

⑤ Click one of these Search Within links to limit the search area.

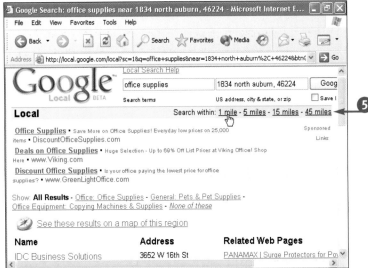

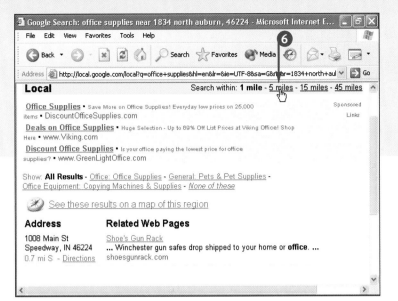

Google refreshes the search results to display only those businesses within the specified mile radius.

*Note: In this case, the 1-mile radius produced only one result.*

6 Click another Search Within link to specify a larger geographical area.

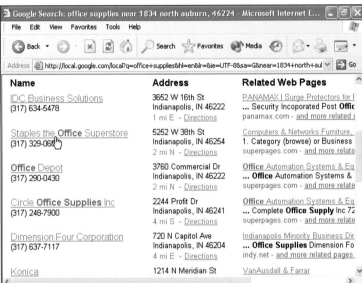

If Google Local finds any businesses that offer the specified product or service within the specified geographical area, it displays them in the search results.

**TIPS**

### More Options!
If Google finds no businesses or organizations that offer the product or service you describe, check your search phrase for misspellings or typographical errors, try different words in your search phrase, or compose a search phrase that is more general.

### Did You Know?
The Search Within links enable you to expand your search to an area with a 45-mile radius. If that still returns no results, Google displays a message with links for further expanding the geographical area.

### Try This!
Below the search results, Google displays the number of pages of search results that it found. If the number exceeds ten pages, consider restricting the search area even further or composing a more specific search phrase to narrow the focus of your search.

# View
# RELATED PAGES

Google Local search results usually contain the names of at least a few businesses or organizations that offer the product or service you describe. However, the search results may contain some entries that are close to what you had in mind but do not exactly meet your needs. In such cases, you may be able to find the right match by checking out related pages.

Whenever Google Local finds a business or organization that has other businesses or organizations in the

same category, it displays them in the Related Web Pages column to the right of the business addresses. You can click the link for a related Web page or click the And More Related Pages link to view a list of pages related to the location. These pages are often the sources from which Google obtained its information about the business or organization. Using these sources, you can often expand your search to other related establishments.

① Perform a Google local search as you normally would.

● Google displays a list of businesses or organizations that offer the product or service you described.

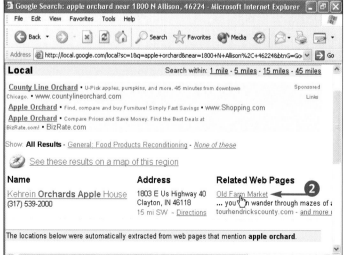

② Click the link for the source site of one of the businesses.

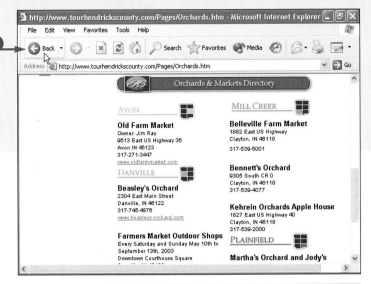

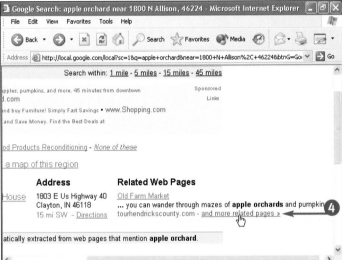

Google Local displays the source from which it obtained the business listing.

**③** Click Back.

**DIFFICULTY LEVEL**

Your browser displays the original list of search results.

**④** Click And More Related Pages.

Google Local displays a map showing the location of the business or organization followed by links to other sources that mention the establishment.

## TIPS

### Did You Know?
The Web houses thousands of specialized directories, and many of these directories are devoted to specific industries. They often supply much more detailed and directed information than you can find using a Web search tool or phone book. The Related Web Pages feature helps you track down these specialized directories.

### Try This!
Perform a new search using keywords from a related Web page. This can often point you in a new, more productive direction.

### Important!
Google makes no guarantee that the search results contain accurate information. Call the business or organization first to confirm that it exists, that the address provided is correct, and that the establishment does in fact offer the product or service you need.

# View search
# RESULTS ON A MAP

Because Google has access to both phone book listings and map services, it can provide what no ordinary phone book offers — a detailed map, showing the location of each and every business and organization in its directory. Whenever you click a link for a business or organization, Google presents a map of the area showing precisely where it is located. You can then zoom in for additional details or zoom out for the big picture view. Google even provides a link that you can click to obtain driving directions, as shown in task #57.

Google does not provide the map itself but links to MapQuest or another online map service to supply the map. The map that appears shows not only the location of the business or organization but also the starting point location you entered. This gives you a general idea of the location of the business or organization in relation to you. The map also provides controls to scroll the map up or down and from side to side to view neighboring areas.

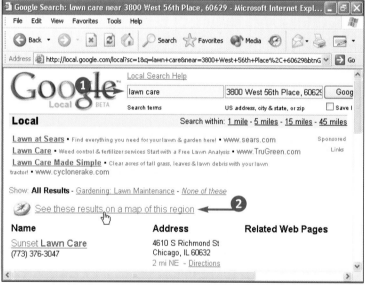

① Perform a Google local search as you normally would.

Google displays a list of businesses or organizations that offer the described product or service.

② Click See These Results on a Map of This Region.

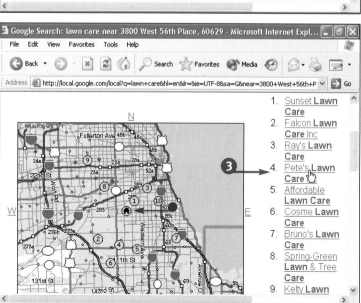

Google displays a map pinpointing the location of the top businesses or organizations in the search results.

● This icon (▣) marks the starting point location you entered.

③ Click the link for a business or organization that looks promising.

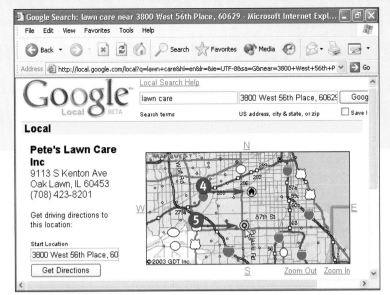

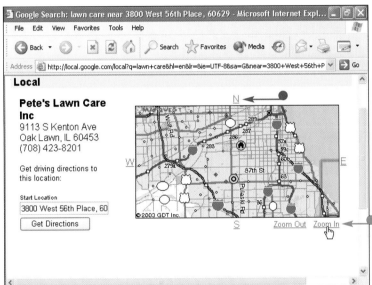

Google displays the name, address, and phone number of the business or organization along with a map showing its location.

④ Note the icon showing your location.

⑤ Find the icon (◎) that pinpoints the location of the business or organization.

**DIFFICULTY LEVEL**

● You can click one of these links to zoom in or out.

● You can click the direction indicators to scroll the map in the direction that you want.

### Try This!

Go to www.yellowpages.com or another online business directory and perform the same search. Note any differences in the results returned. In most cases, Google provides results that rival those of an online business directory.

### Did You Know?

You can go to Google's home page at www.google.com and enter an address complete with a city and state or zip code to have Google display a phone directory listing for the business or residence. See task #23 for details.

### More Options!

If Google finds other businesses in the same category as a business you searched for, it may display a link above the map and below the Local bar to search for other similar businesses in the area.

# Obtain
# DRIVING DIRECTIONS

Knowing where a business is located and knowing how to get there from a particular departure point are two different things. If you pull up a map and are unfamiliar with an area, you can ask Google for directions. You already entered your current location, so Google knows your departure point. As soon as you select a business or organization, Google knows your destination point. When you click the button to get directions, Google passes the departure and destination point addresses to an online map service, which then generates the directions.

Occasionally, the map service requires some clarification or additional information about the departure or destination points before it can route you to your destination. When the map service requires additional information, it displays a screen requesting the information or requesting confirmation of information it has already gleaned from the information you provided. Simply enter the additional information or click the button to confirm, and the online map service displays the driving directions. In addition, the service typically displays the distance and an estimate of travel time.

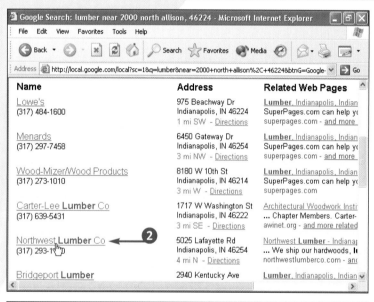

① Perform a Google local search as you normally would.

Google displays a list of businesses or organizations that offer the described product or service.

② Click the link for a business or organization that you want to locate.

Google Local displays the name, address, and phone number of the business or organization along with a map.

● The address you entered as your starting point appears here. You can edit it.

③ Click Get Directions.

- If the online map service needs additional information or a confirmation, it displays a request.

④ Enter any additional information, as needed.

⑤ Click Get Directions.

**DIFFICULTY LEVEL**

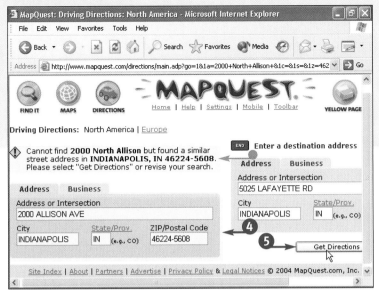

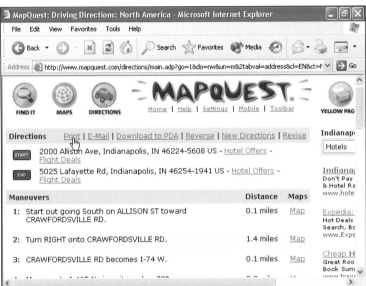

The map service displays directions from the point of departure to the destination.

## Did You Know?

Most map services display a screen version of the directions that contain additional information you do not need. Instead of choosing Print from the File menu, look for a Print option on the page. This typically displays a printable version of the map and directions without extraneous content, such as sponsor links.

## Try This!

If you keep track of mileage for business purposes, use the mileage estimate that the map service provides if you often forget to keep track of odometer readings. To record mileage, simply note on your calendar when you drove to a particular destination and jot down the mileage that the map service provided. Make sure that you multiply the distance by 2 for round trips.

# Change your
# SAVED LOCATION

Having Google Local save the location that you entered can save you time when you perform new searches. But what happens if you move? Or, if you are planning a vacation to a different city and want to check out the local scene there, how do you change your location?

Fortunately, Google makes changing locations very easy. When you enter a location and click the check box to save it, Google places a cookie on your computer, which acts as a badge that identifies your computer when you return to Google. After

you click the check box to save your location and then perform a search, Google saves the address you entered and clears the check box. You can change your location when you perform your next search, as shown in this task.

You can clear your address completely by deleting your address from the location text box and choosing to save the location. Or you can click the Local Search Help link and click a link in the FAQs to remove the address.

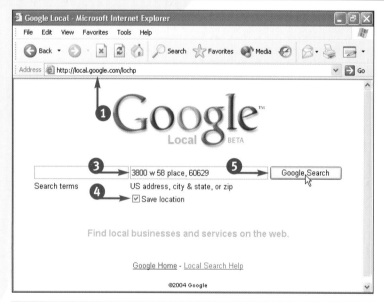

## CHANGE YOUR LOCATION

① Type **local.google.com** and press Enter.

Google Local appears.

② Highlight the entry in the location box.

③ Type the new address that you want to use.

④ Click Save Location (☐ changes to ☑ ).

⑤ Click Google Search.

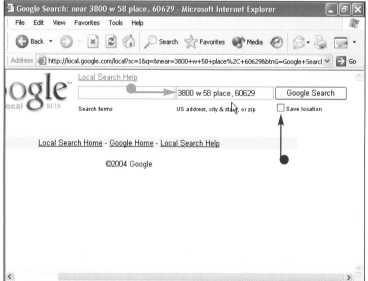

● Google Local saves the new address.

● Google clears the Save Location check box to indicate that it saved the new address.

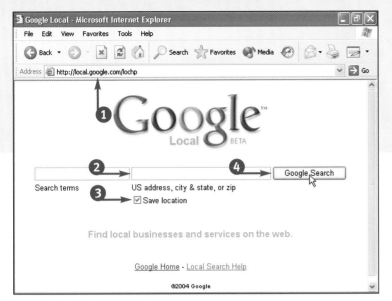

① Type **local.google.com** and press Enter.

Google Local appears.

② Delete the entry in the location box.

③ Click Save Location (☐ changes to ☑).

④ Click Google Search.

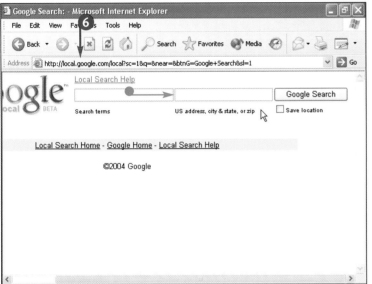

⑤ Exit and restart your Web browser.

⑥ Type **local.google.com** and press Enter.

● The location box is blank.

## Attention!
If you change or delete the location address but do not exit and restart your Web browser, the original address appears in the location box when you go to Google Local. You must exit and restart your Web browser so that it clears the information stored in the cookie that identifies your browser to Google Local.

## More Options!
Every Google Local screen contains a Local Search Help link, typically near the top or bottom of the screen. Click Local Search Help to learn more about Google Local and to access a link you can click to remove your address from the location box. However, even if you use the link to remove your address, you must exit and restart your browser for the change to take effect.

# Correct a listing for
# YOUR BUSINESS

When business owners become aware that Google reaches millions of potential consumers every day, they quickly develop an interest in having their businesses listed on Google — and listed correctly. If you own your own business, you probably have already searched Google to find your listing. If your business relies a great deal on local clientele, you should also perform a Google local search to see if your business is listed and what the listing contains.

What if you own a flower shop in Detroit that Google Local does not list when you search for "flowers" in

your zip code? You could be missing out on opportunities to sell flowers to hundreds of people in your area alone. Is there anything you can do about it? Yes, you can contact Google via e-mail, as shown in this task.

Google is not actually the service responsible for omissions. Google gathers its information from *Yellow Pages* sources, which contain the original listings. However, you can send an e-mail request to Google to have Google pass the information along to its sources.

① Type **local.google.com** and press Enter.

Google Local appears.

② Scroll down the page and click Local Search Help.

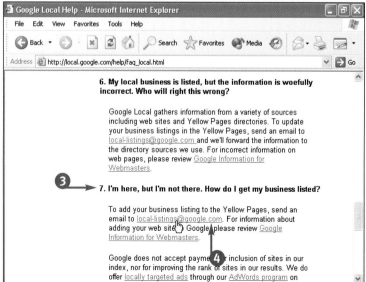

Google displays its Local Search Help screen.

③ Scroll down the page to the FAQs for correcting omissions and errors.

④ Click the link for notifying Google Local of errors or omissions via e-mail.

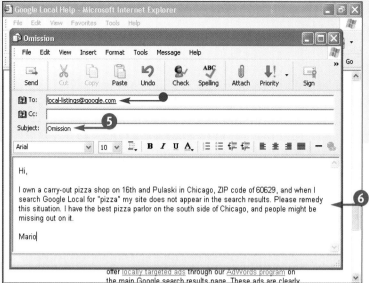

- Your e-mail program runs and opens a new message window addressed to local-listings@google.com.

⑤ Type a message description.

⑥ Type your message informing Google Local of the error or omission.

⑦ Click Send.

Your computer sends the e-mail message to Google Local, which then forwards it to the responsible party.

## TIPS

### Important!
Do not expect immediate action on your message. Google and its sources must verify the information that you submitted. The source must then correct the information that it has stored in its database and then make this information available to Google. The process can take several weeks.

### Important!
Provide Google with as much detail as you can. What subject did you search for, expecting your business listing to appear? What sorts of products and services does your business provide? Perhaps your business is listed in the wrong category. This information helps Google's source create a more accurate listing and ensure placement in the proper category.

### More Options!
If you notice any other problems with the Google Local service, you can notify Google Local at local-help@google.com.

# CREATE GOOGLE ADWORDS
## for your business

Web authors constantly explore methods to make Google and other search engines list their Web sites higher in the search results so that they can achieve more visibility on the Web. One sure way that you can make your business more visible is to create Google AdWords for your business.

As a Google user, you probably have already encountered Google ads. These are the sponsor links that appear on the right side of the page when you perform a Google search and appear at the top of the page when you perform a Google Local search.

Perhaps you have even clicked a Google ad link to order a product or service online.

You can create a Google ad to advertise your products and services, as well. Creating an ad is fairly simple and takes less than 15 minutes. You create the ad yourself, right online; specify the keywords you want Google to use to match your ad with search words that other Google users enter and specify the countries or regions where you want your ad to appear. Google charges a fee only when a user clicks your ad.

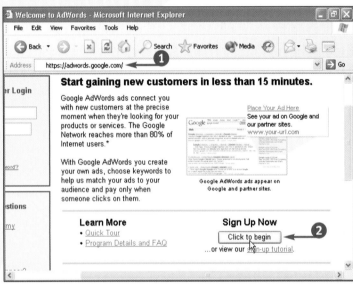

① Type **adwords.google.com** and press Enter.

② Click Click to Begin.

Google starts to lead you through the process of creating and targeting your ad.

③ Follow the on-screen instructions to target your ad to a specific country and region.

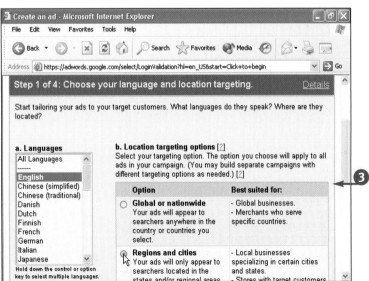

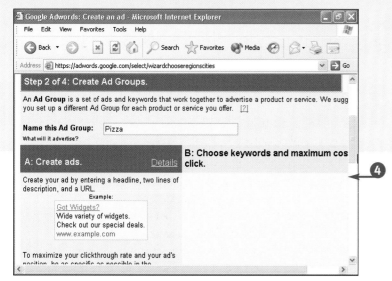

Next, Google leads you through the process of creating an ad.

**#60**

4 Follow the on-screen instructions to create an ad and specify the address of the page that appears when a user clicks your ad.

**DIFFICULTY LEVEL**

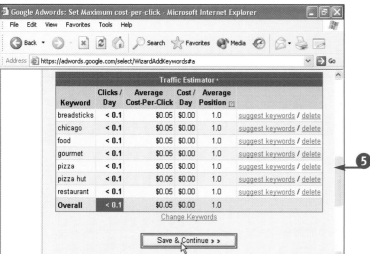

Next, Google leads you through the process of establishing a daily budget and entering your account information.

5 Follow the on-screen instructions to specify a spending limit and create a Google ad account.

Google activates your ad, so it appears when users enter the keywords that you specified.

**TIPS**

### Important!
Google calculates your charge based on cost per click (CPC), which can range from 5 cents to $50. You choose a maximum CPC, which determines your position in the sponsored links. When you enter a CPC, Google also provides an estimate of the amount of traffic that you can expect. For more information about cost and billing, go to adwords.google.com/support.

### Did You Know?
Google Network is an advertising network that includes *The New York Times,* America Online, and Netscape Netcenter. Your ads can potentially appear at these sites, as well.

### Remove It!
You can remove an ad at any time. Go to adwords.google.com, log in to your account, click the check box next to the ad campaign that you want to remove (☐ changes to ☑ ), and click Delete.

# Chapter 7

# Save Money with Google's Froogle

Froogle is Google's online shopping directory that enables you to search for specific products and services. With Froogle, you can save money by searching thousands of competing merchants and narrowing your search to a particular price range. Froogle is most useful for tracking down the lowest prices for a specific item, such as a DVD or video game, but it can help you find a wide range of products and services.

Froogle's search index obtains its results from two sources — its search robots that constantly wander the Web looking for sites and information that various merchants automatically feed to Froogle. This provides you and other users with a thorough index of products and services.

Like a basic Google Web search, Froogle offers several methods for searching and various

ways of presenting the search results. You can select the way Froogle lists products, sort products by price, limit your search to a particular price range, group results by store, or browse by category, as if you were shopping in a department store.

Froogle does not charge merchants for better placement or receive compensation if you choose to order a product that you find through Froogle. After you find a product at a price that appeals to you, you click the link to connect to the merchant's site and then deal directly with the merchant to order the product or service.

At the writing of this book, Froogle was in the Beta testing phase, so "Beta" appears on many of the screens in this chapter.

# Top 100

# SEARCH FROOGLE
## for a product or service

The Froogle search page is nearly identical to the Google search page, and you can use it to search for products in almost exactly the same way that you perform a Google search. The only difference between a Froogle and Google search is that Froogle restricts its search results to product and merchant sites.

As with a Google search, Froogle displays its results in two columns. The column on the left displays an automatically generated list of results with the

results that Froogle deems most relevant at the top of the list. Merchants cannot pay for better placement on this list. The column on the right displays links to sponsor sites. Links in this column take you to merchant sites that pay Google to list their sites when users enter specific keywords in a search.

When searching Froogle, you can use many of the same search operators that you use to search Google. Refer to Chapter 1 for details.

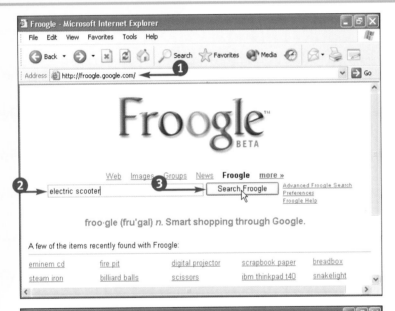

① Type **froogle.google.com** and press Enter.

② Type one or more words describing the product or service that you want.

③ Click Search Froogle.

Froogle displays a photo and brief description of any products or services it finds matching your description.

④ Scroll to the right, if necessary, to view links to sponsor sites, where you can find the item and shop for similar items.

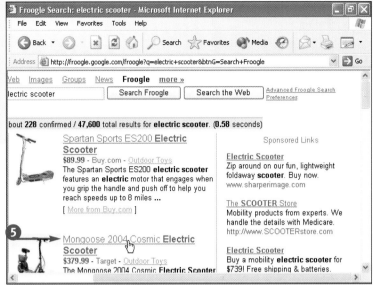

Your browser displays the merchant page that contains the listing.

## More Options!

A standard Froogle search, like the one shown in this task, typically provides an overabundance of results sorted in no useful order. Refer to other tasks in this chapter to learn how to perform an advanced search, sort results by price or by store, set a price range, change views, and specify other preferences.

## Did You Know?

Froogle attempts to determine a price and category for each item that it lists. If Froogle cannot determine a price or category for items that match your description, it separates those results from the other results using a horizontal line.

## Try This!

Enclose your search phrase in quotes to find only those items that match your phrase exactly as typed. To exclude descriptions that contain a particular word, type a hyphen before the word.

# Perform an
# ADVANCED FROOGLE SEARCH

Unless you specify otherwise, Froogle performs a broad search to display the most listings that match your search description. If you are searching for rare items, such as antiques or memorabilia, this may be exactly the type of search that you want to perform. However, if you want a fairly common product or service from a reputable company for the best price possible, the standard search results are not very useful.

You can have Froogle display more targeted search results by performing an advanced search. From

Froogle's Advanced Search page, you can specify that Froogle search for descriptions that contain your search phrase exactly as you type it, that contain any of the words you typed, or that do not contain certain words. You can also specify where you want Froogle to look for the search phrase — in the product name or description, or in both.

With an advanced search, you can specify a price range, limit your search to a specific category, group the results by store, display the results in grid view, and even filter out potentially offensive results.

① Type **froogle.google.com** and press Enter.

② Click Advanced Froogle Search.

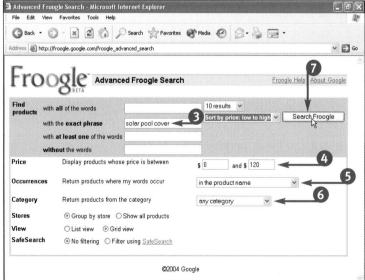

The Advanced Froogle Search screen appears.

③ Type a description of the product or service.

④ Type the price range that you want.

⑤ Click here and select where to look for the description that you typed.

⑥ Click here and select the shopping category that you want.

⑦ Click Search Froogle.

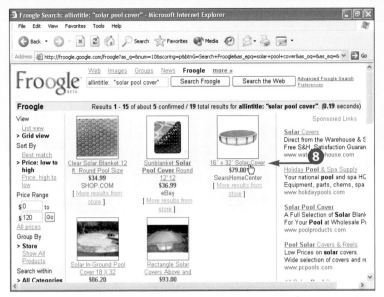

Froogle displays items that match your search word or words.

⑧ Click the item that you want.

**DIFFICULTY LEVEL**

The merchant's Web site opens and displays the selected item.

● You can click the link for ordering the item online.

**TIPS**

## More Options!

Google has a huge collection of catalogs. To access a store's catalog, go to froogle.google.com, click the More link, click the Catalogs link, and follow the links to the catalog that you want. A store's catalog consists of scanned catalog pages, which do not support online ordering.

## Did You Know?

If you have a business and want to know if your products or services are listed on Froogle, do a search and see. If your product is not listed, you can submit a data feed to Froogle with a complete list of products and services. Click the Information for Merchants link at the bottom of the Froogle screen for more information, and refer to task #70.

# Change
# LISTING VIEWS

DIFFICULTY LEVEL

By default, Froogle's search results include a photo and a brief description, if available, of each product or service that matches your search entry. The description can be very useful in helping you choose an item, but it consumes a great deal of window space. You can display more products per screen by hiding the descriptions in Froogle's Grid view. The Grid view displays a limited amount of information about each item listed, including a photo, if available, a link to the site where you can order the item, the listed price, and a link to the merchant site.

## TIPS

### Did You Know?
If you perform an advanced search, as shown in task #62, you can choose to have the results returned in the Grid or List view.

### Remove It!
You can switch from the Grid view back to the original display, which is called List view. To do so, click the List view link, just above the Grid View link.

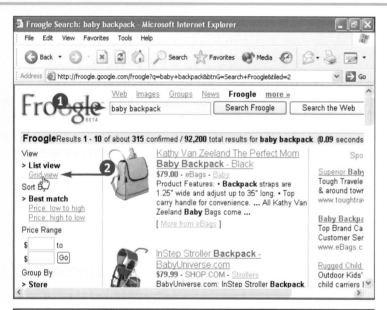

① Search Froogle for a product or service as you normally would.

*Note: See task #61 or #62 for Froogle search instructions.*

② Click Grid View.

Google displays the search results in the Grid view, with more results per page.

# Sort by PRICE

You can take full advantage of Froogle by using it to shop for products and services at the best prices. You can do this in two ways — by specifying a price range, as shown in task #65, or by having Froogle sort the search results by price, as shown in this task. You can sort the results from lowest to highest price, which is most common, or from highest to lowest. You may choose to sort from highest to lowest to have higher-quality items listed first, assuming of course that price indicates quality. You can do both — limit your search to a particular price range and have Froogle sort the results by price.

If you perform an advanced Froogle search, as shown in task #62, you can choose to sort by price before you execute your search. If you have already performed a search, you can click one of the Sort By links on the results page to have Froogle sort the results from lowest to highest or highest to lowest price.

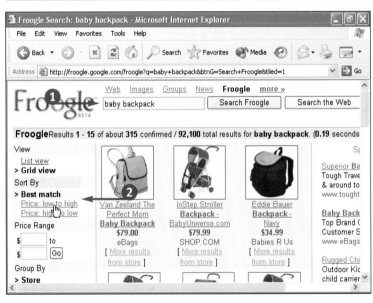

① Search Froogle for a product or service as you normally would.

*Note: See task #61 or #62 for Froogle search instructions.*

② Click Price: Low to High or Price: High to Low.

Froogle rearranges the search items to display them in the specified order.

# Limit results to a
# PRICE RANGE

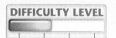

When shopping, most people have a particular price range in mind or at least an upper price limit beyond which they are unwilling to pay. If you have a price range in mind, you can enter it in Froogle to narrow the selection of items.

If you perform an advanced search, as shown in task #62, you can specify a price range before you execute your search. The Advanced Froogle Search form contains two price amount boxes, so you can enter a lower and upper limit. If you perform a standard Froogle search, as shown in task #61, you

can add a price range to your description. For example, you can type **nikon coolpix $250..300** to have Froogle find Nikon COOLPIX cameras ranging in price from $250 to $300.

You can also enter a price range after you perform a search. If the search results contain thousands of entries, for example, you can quickly limit the results by entering a price range and re-executing the search.

---

① Search Froogle for a product or service as you normally would.

*Note: See task #61 or #62 for Froogle search instructions.*

② Click here and type a lowest price limit.

③ Click here and type a highest price limit.

④ Click Go.

Froogle displays only those products or services that fall within your price range.

# Show
# ALL RESULTS

**DIFFICULTY LEVEL**

By default, Froogle groups the search results by store, displaying one item from each merchant. Following the description of the item is a More from *Store Name* link that you can click to view more items that the merchant carries. Grouping items by store provides you with a wider selection of shopping options, but it hides items that you may be looking for just because a particular merchant already has one item listed.

You can turn off the Group by Store option by clicking the Show All Products link. When you choose to show all products, Froogle returns the same

number of listings, but it reorganizes the list to show those items that are most relevant to your search, regardless of which store carries the items. For example, if you search for "perfume," Froogle may display five links to products at Wal-Mart at the very top of the list. With Group by Store selected, Froogle would display only one product from Wal-Mart.

Selecting the Show All Products link is particularly useful if only one or two specialty shops carry the item that you want.

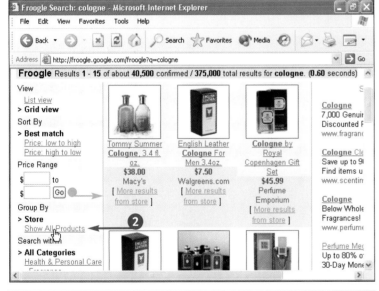

1 Search Froogle for a product or service as you normally would.

*Note: See task #61 or #62 for Froogle search instructions.*

● Notice that each store has only one product listed.

2 Click Show All Products.

● Google displays all products, regardless of whether a merchant carries one or more of them.

# Limit results by
# CATEGORY

DIFFICULTY LEVEL

Froogle's search results often contain items from categories that you do not want to include in your search. For example, if you search for a book by its title and a video with the same title is also available, Froogle includes the video in the search results. The search results may even include posters and other items of the same name. You can limit your search to a particular category to filter out these extraneous items.

By performing an advanced search, as shown in task #62, you can select a category to limit your search. However, the categories that the Froogle Advanced

Search page offers are fairly broad. The Books, Music, & Video category, for example, would do you little good in excluding soundtracks and videos from a search for books.

To more effectively restrict your search to a particular category, you can perform the search and then click the name of the category that you want. Froogle displays a category link next to each item in the results list. It also displays a list of categories in the left column.

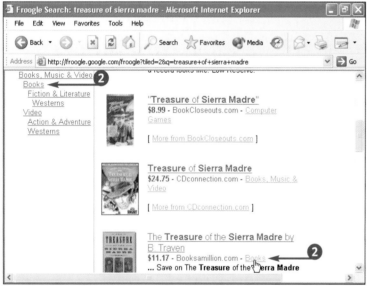

① Search Froogle for a product or service that is likely to be listed in more than one category.

*Note: See task #61 or #62 for Froogle search instructions.*

② Click the category link next to an item or in the list of categories on the left.

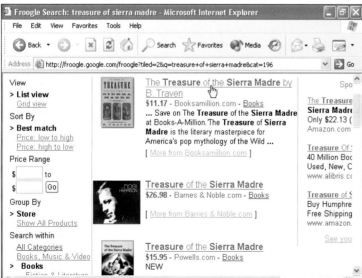

Google displays new search results limited to items in the selected category.

# Browse
# GOOGLE CATEGORIES

When you are shopping, you may not know exactly what you want or need, especially when you are shopping for "the perfect gift." With Froogle, you can start shopping even if you do not have a specific product or service in mind. You can pull up a list of Froogle categories and then follow the categories and subcategories to shop for various types of products or services. Froogle's categories include Apparel & Accessories, Art & Entertainment, Babies, Computers, Flowers, and Home & Garden.

Early versions of Froogle displayed the categories at the bottom of the Froogle search page. During the

writing of this book, Froogle was still in the Beta testing phase. The bottom of the Froogle search page contained links to search for commonly searched for items but provided no clear way to pull up the categories. This task shows how to display the categories by performing an advanced search with no product or service description. However, Google may decide to return the categories to the Froogle search page or provide a link to the categories by the time it finalizes Froogle.

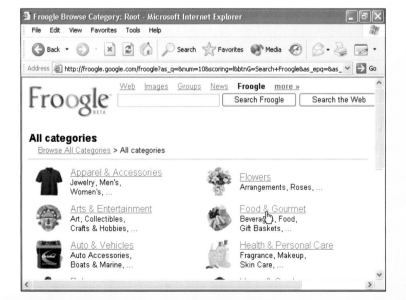

1 Display the Advanced Froogle Search page.

*Note: For more information about an advanced Froogle search, see task #62.*

2 Leave the search boxes blank.

3 Click here and select Any Category.

4 Click Search Froogle.

Froogle displays its categories, which you can click to browse for products and services.

# MERCHANT SITE

Although Froogle may look and function like an electronic shopping mall, it is actually more of a referral service. Froogle helps you track down products and services, but as soon as you click a link, you leave Froogle to go directly to the merchant's site, where you can obtain additional information about the item and perhaps shop for other items or order items online. Froogle does not guarantee that a particular business is legitimate or that it offers reliable products or services.

Jumping to a merchant site is easy. When you have found the product or service that you want, click its link, as shown in this task.

Like Google, every Froogle search page contains a list of sponsor links on the right side of the page. Sponsor links link to merchant pages that pay Google to have their sites displayed on search pages. Unlike the product links that a search returns, which Froogle sorts by relevance, sponsor links owe their positions, in large part, to the amount of money the merchants pay for placement.

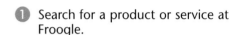

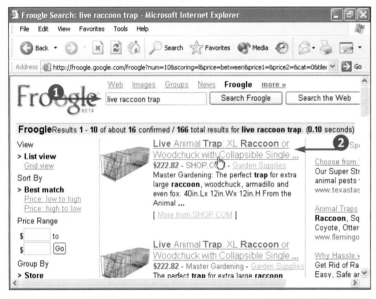

① Search for a product or service at Froogle.

*Note: See task #61 or #62 for Froogle search instructions.*

② Click the link for a product or service that you want.

Your browser displays the product page at the merchant's site.

# MERCHANT INFORMATION #70

The Froogle directory obtains its listings from two sources — Google search robots and data feeds from various merchants. If you own a business and your products or services do not show up, or the listing displays inaccurate information when you search Froogle, your company may not have a strong Web presence or may not be feeding Froogle the necessary information.

To ensure that your products and services are listed correctly, you can set up a data feed to pass your product information to Froogle. Froogle provides a

page dedicated exclusively to merchants that provides answers to frequently asked questions and instructions on how to set up the necessary data feeds.

Froogle provides easy access to merchant information by placing a link to the merchant information page at the bottom of every Froogle search page. If you would like to have your business show up in the list of sponsored links, you can create a Google ad for your business, as shown in task #60.

**DIFFICULTY LEVEL**

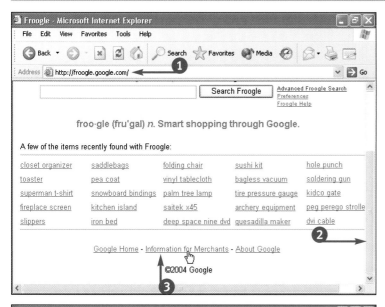

① Type **froogle.google.com** and press Enter.

② Scroll down to the bottom of the page.

③ Click Information for Merchants.

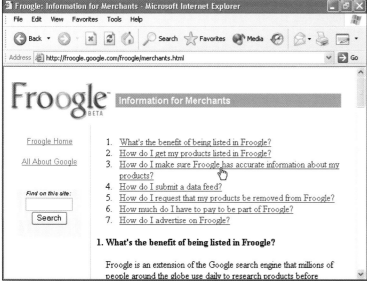

Froogle displays a list of frequently asked questions for business owners.

# Chapter 8

# Read and Post Messages in Discussion Forums

Usenet, short for *User's network,* is an online bulletin board system, where users from all over the world can post their own messages and read messages from other users. Usenet consists of tens of thousands of electronic bulletin boards that cover every topic imaginable — from technical support to politics, from pet care to body art, and from auto maintenance to entrepreneurial opportunities.

In the not-so-distant past, you needed a *newsgroup reader,* such as Outlook Express or Netscape Mail & Newsgroups, to access newsgroups, read messages, and post messages to newsgroups. Newsgroup readers provided few tools for finding specific newsgroups, so you had to do some savvy detective work to track down a specific newsgroup and find messages that pertained to your interests or needs.

Google Groups offers an alternative to newsgroup readers, providing a searchable archive of nearly a billion newsgroup postings dating back to 1981. Google Groups provides two significant advantages over traditional newsgroup readers: It makes newsgroups accessible from any Web browser anywhere in the world, and it provides a searchable index of posted messages. In addition, you can browse Google groups by newsgroup category. The only real drawback to Google Groups is that it does not enable you to post files or access files that other users have posted to a newsgroup.

This chapter introduces you to Google Groups and provides tips that show you how to take full advantage of Google Groups searches. In addition, you learn how to read and post messages, locate a message you posted, and delete messages you posted by mistake.

# Top 100

# Browse all
# GOOGLE GROUPS

Google Groups provides a directory of Usenet newsgroups, which you can browse by newsgroup type and topic. The opening Google Groups screen lists the various types of newsgroups, including alt (alternative), biz (business) comp (computer), and rec (recreation). When you click a general newsgroup category, Google Groups displays a list of newsgroups and newsgroup subcategories that you can explore.

By default, Google Groups displays 50 newsgroups and subcategories at a time. Just above the list,

Google Groups displays a link that you can click to view the next 50 newsgroups and subcategories. Google Groups also provides a drop-down list that enables you to skip to a specific subcategory. Because each newsgroup category contains thousands of individual newsgroups, you can save a great deal of time by learning to quickly navigate to a particular subcategory. By learning how to zero in on a specific category, you can save time later when you search for specific newsgroups because Google Groups enables you to limit your search to a specific category or newsgroup.

① Type **www.google.com** and press Enter.

② Click Groups.

The Google Groups home page appears.

③ Click the newsgroup category that you want.

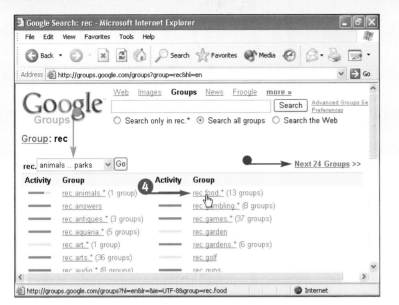

A list of newsgroups and subcategories in the selected category appears.

● You can click here to see the next group of newsgroups and subcategories.

● You can click here and select a subgroup.

④ Click the subcategory that you want.

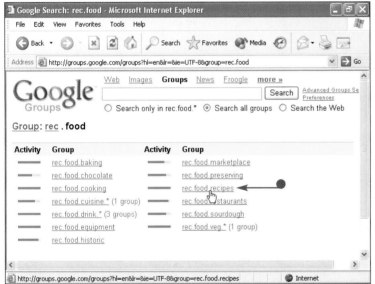

Google Groups displays the newsgroups in the selected subcategory.

● You can click a newsgroup's link to display its messages.

## TIPS

### More Options!
The opening Google Groups page displays a very limited selection of newsgroup categories. To view a complete list of newsgroup categories, click the Browse Complete List of Groups link that follows the limited list of categories.

### More Options!
By default, Google Groups uses moderate SafeSearch filtering to screen out any potentially offensive newsgroups. You can change the SafeSearch filtering setting and other Google Groups settings by clicking the Preferences link on the opening Google Groups page. Even with SafeSearch filtering enabled, you can expect to see some potentially offensive postings.

### Did You Know?
Google provides a lot of background information and specific instructions about using Google Groups. On the opening page, click the Groups Help link.

# Search Google Groups for
# SPECIFIC TOPICS

Given that Google Groups archives nearly a billion newsgroup messages, you can imagine how difficult locating a message that addresses a specific topic may be. Fortunately, Google Groups leverages the power of Google's search tools to help you track down messages that address specific topics.

This task shows you how to perform a standard Google Groups search from the opening window. Task #73 shows how to perform a more targeted search using the Google Groups Advanced Search option. However, as this task shows, you can find plenty of messages that address a specific topic by performing

a standard search. In addition, Google Groups displays a number of links as part of its search results that you can use to jump directly to a particular newsgroup and browse or search that newsgroup for the message that you want. You can also gain access to sponsor links that may lead to Web sites where you can learn more about the topic you searched.

If the topic is time sensitive, you can sort the results by date, which lists the most-recently posted messages at the top.

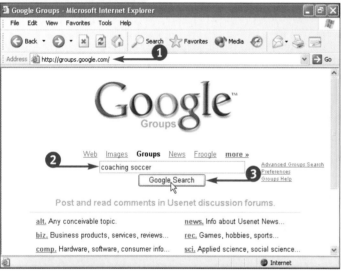

① Type **groups.google.com** and press Enter.

Google Groups appears.

② Type one or more words to describe the topic in which you are interested.

③ Click Google Search.

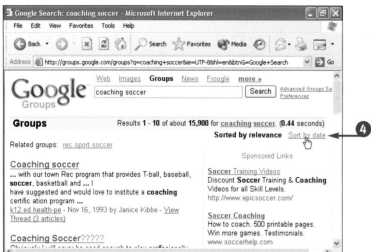

Google displays a list of links to messages that match your description.

④ Click Sort by Date.

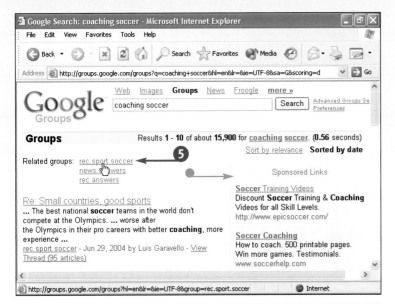

# 72

Google rearranges the list of results to place the most currently posted messages at the top.

● Sponsor links appear here.

❺ Click the link for the newsgroup that you want.

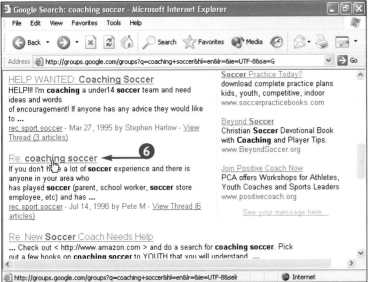

Google Groups displays only the messages posted to that newsgroup.

❻ Click the link for the message that you want to read.

Your browser displays the contents of the selected message.

## More Options!

You can type your search phrase enclosed in quotation marks to have Google Groups search for only messages that contain your search phrase exactly as you typed it. However, if your search phrase contains any common words, such as *the* or *to*, Google Groups drops the word from the phrase. To have Google Groups include a common word, type a plus sign before the word. Google Groups displays any dropped words in the Groups bar that appears just above the search results.

## Remove It!

If you click the Sort by Date link to place more recent messages at the top of the list, you can return to the original listing by clicking the Sort by Relevance link.

## Did You Know?

Following the description of each message is a link to the newsgroup in which the message was posted.

# Perform an
# ADVANCED GOOGLE GROUPS SEARCH

Searching for newsgroup messages from the Google Groups opening page often returns a list of search results that is too general and too lengthy to be of much use. You can get more targeted results by performing an advanced search.

The Google Groups Advanced Search page features several options for narrowing or broadening a search. You can specify that the search results include only messages that contain your search phrase exactly as you typed it, include messages that contain *any* of the words in your search phrase, or exclude messages that contain a particular word or phrase.

You can specify the newsgroup or newsgroups that you want to search, limit the search results to those messages posted by a specific author or composed in a specific language, filter out potentially offensive messages, and limit your search to messages posted in a given date range. You can also have the search results sorted by date or by relevance, which is the default sort order.

This task shows you how to access the Advanced Search page and use it to search for messages.

① Type **groups.google.com** and press Enter.

② Click Advanced Groups Search.

The Advanced Groups Search page appears.

③ Type your search phrase in one or more of the Find Messages boxes to describe the message for which you are looking.

④ Click here and select the number of messages to return.

⑤ Click here and select the sort order that you want.

## 73

**DIFFICULTY LEVEL**

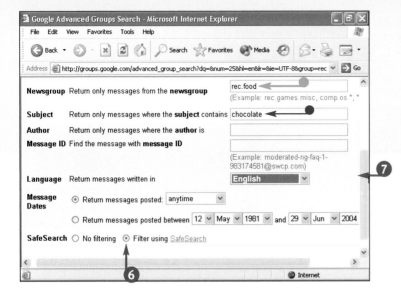

- You can limit the search to a specific newsgroup.

- You can search for messages that include a word or phrase in the subject line.

⑥ Click here to filter out potentially offensive messages.

⑦ Enter any additional search preferences, as needed.

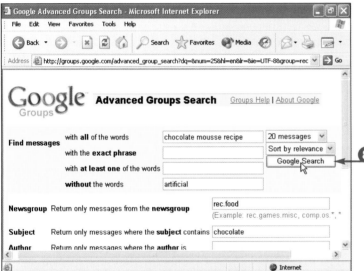

⑧ Click Google Search.

If Google finds any messages that match your search instructions, it displays links to those messages.

## Try This!

Open the Google Groups opening page at groups.google.com. Using the Google Groups categories, as shown in task #71, navigate to the newsgroup that you want to search. Just below the search box, click the Search Only In option ( ○ changes to ⊙ ) for the currently selected newsgroup. Then click the Advanced Groups Search link. This inserts the newsgroup's name in the Return Only Messages from the Newsgroup box, so you do not need to type it.

## Did You Know?

Most newsgroup messages have an ID number that you can use to find the message. Users may refer to particularly useful messages by ID number when posting a reply to another user who requests help. You can use the Google Groups Advanced Search options to search for messages by ID.

# Display
# MESSAGE CONTENTS

Whether you navigate through a list of newsgroups and newsgroup categories or perform a standard or advanced search, you will eventually encounter one or more messages that address a topic or question of interest. Intuitively, you know to click the link for that message to display its contents. This displays a message window that may not appear so intuitive.

At the top of the message window is the message header, which is text that any newsgroup reader can append to the top of a posted message. The header typically includes the subject or title of the post, the

name and e-mail address of the person who posted the message, the date and time it was posted, and so on.

Below the header, you may see what appears to be the message, but each line begins with an angle bracket (>). The angle bracket is a standard way of showing that these lines are quoted from a previously posted message — the message to which this message replies.

Finally, below the quoted message is the contents of the message that you chose to read.

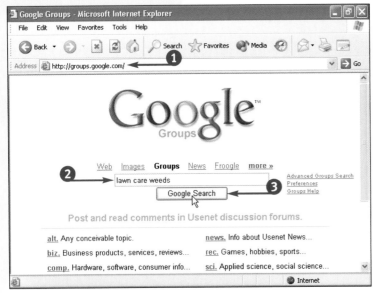

① Type **groups.google.com** and press Enter.

The Google Groups opening page appears.

② Type one or more words describing the message that you are looking for.

③ Click Google Search.

Google displays links to messages that match your description.

④ Click the link for the message that you want to read.

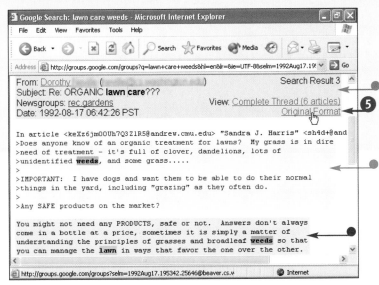

Google displays the contents of the selected message.

- This is the newsgroup message header.

- This is the quoted message.

- This is the contents of the message that you selected to read.

**5** Click Original Format.

## 74

**DIFFICULTY LEVEL**

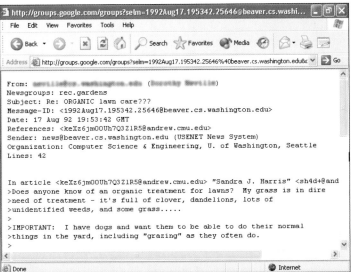

Google Groups displays the message without the Google Groups formatting applied.

## TIPS

### More Options!

When you click a link to view a message that is part of an ongoing discussion, Google Groups displays only the selected message. You can click the View Thread link to view all the messages that compose the discussion. For more information, see task #75.

### Remove It!

If you click the Original Format link to view the plain text version of a posted message and want to return to the version that has Google Groups formatting applied to it, click your Web browser's Back button.

### Did You Know?

The message header that appears above the contents of the message includes a link to the newsgroup in which the message was posted. You can click the link to display a list of messages recently posted to that newsgroup.

# Follow a
# DISCUSSION THREAD

When Google Groups displays a list of messages, you can click a message's link to display its contents. If the discussion consists of a single message, Google Groups displays the contents of the message along with links pointing to the newsgroup or newsgroups in which the message was posted, a link to the author that you can click to view links to other messages that the author posted, and a link for posting a reply to this message.

If you click the View Thread link, which accompanies each message that is part of an ongoing discussion —

a discussion that consists of an original message and one or more replies — Google Groups displays the entire *discussion thread* in a separate frame it creates on the left side of your Web browser's window. A discussion thread is the entire discussion, consisting of the original message and any replies. You can click a link in the discussion thread to display the contents of the selected message in the message frame on the right side of the window.

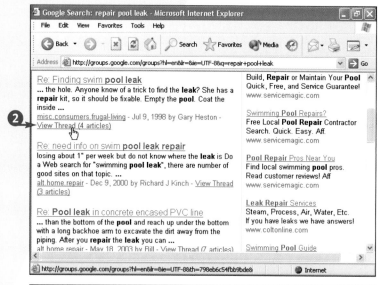

① Display a list of links to messages.

**Note:** *Refer to tasks #71, #72, and #73 for information on finding links to messages.*

② Click View Thread to view the entire discussion.

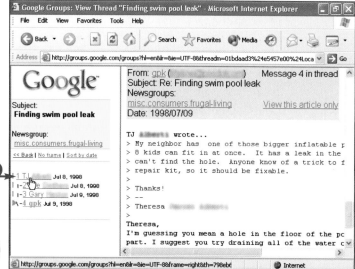

Google Groups displays the discussion thread in the left frame and the contents of the selected message in the right frame.

③ Click the topmost link in the discussion thread to view the first message of the thread.

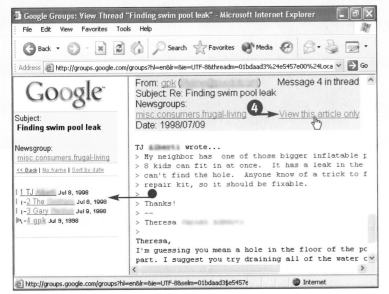

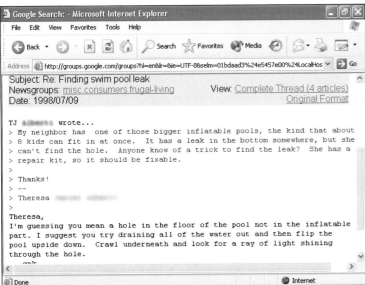

Google Groups displays the contents of the message that initiated the discussion.

● You can click a link for any message in the thread.

④ When you find the message you want to read, click View This Article Only.

**DIFFICULTY LEVEL**

Google closes the discussion thread frame and displays the message in your main browser window.

## TIPS

### More Options!

Just above the discussion thread, Google Groups displays several links: Back, No Frame, and Sort by Date. Click the Back link to display the previous page. Click the Sort by Date link to sort the messages in the thread by date only. Click the No Frame link to hide the discussion frame. If you choose to hide the frame, you can bring it back by clicking the View with Frames link.

### Did You Know?

You can sort the messages in the discussion thread by date or by reply, which makes little difference. Both sort options generally arrange the messages by date. However, the default option, Sort by Reply, provides some indication of which message each message replies to. In many cases, replies are posted to replies rather than as a response to the original message. Sorting by reply provides a clearer sense of context.

# POST A REPLY
## to a message

To provide some control over who can post messages and add a degree of accountability to messages posted from Google Groups, Google requires that you register for access before you can post a reply to any messages or post any original messages to newsgroups. Registering provides you with a screen name that identifies you to Google Groups and to other Usenet users who read and post messages. When you register, you also supply an e-mail address that other Usenet users can employ to send replies to you directly. You can register for Google Groups by

going to www.google.com/accounts.

After you register for Google Groups, you can sign in to your account to gain full access to Google Groups. When you are signed in, you can send replies to posted messages, as shown in this task, and post original messages to begin your own discussions, as shown in task #77. When you post a message, your Google username and the e-mail address you entered to register are posted along with the message so that other users can contact you directly.

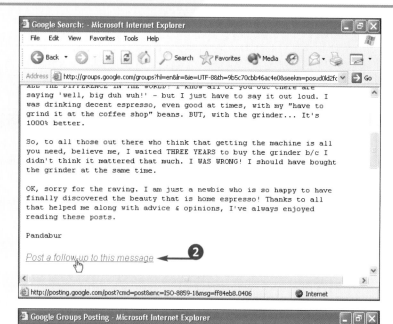

**①** Display a message to which you want to reply.

*Note: For instructions on displaying messages, see task #74.*

**②** Click Post a Follow-up to This Message.

The Compose Your Message page appears with the Send to Group and Subject box already completed.

● You can click here to have a copy of your posted message e-mailed to you.

**③** Delete all but a select portion of the quoted message.

*Note: Leave only enough quoted message to provide a logical context for your reply.*

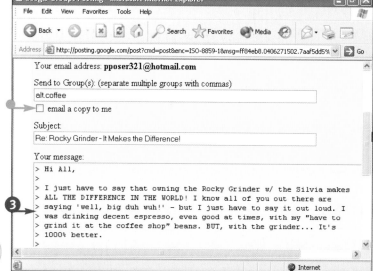

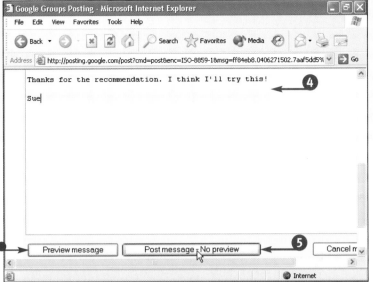

④ Type your reply here.

● You can preview the message before posting it.

⑤ Click Post Message – No Preview.

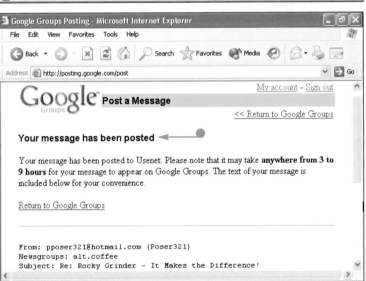

● Google Groups posts your message to the selected newsgroup and includes it as part of the discussion thread.

*Note: Your message may not appear in Google Groups for several hours.*

---

## TIPS

### Important!
The Post a Follow-up to This Message link appears only for messages that are less than one month old. You can read posted messages back to 1981, but you can respond only to fairly current messages.

### Did You Know?
If you are not signed in to Google Groups and you attempt to post a message or a reply, Google displays the page for logging in or registering for Google Groups.

### Caution!
Google requires that you enter a valid e-mail address to post messages. However, you should avoid using your main e-mail address because spammers can obtain your e-mail address from your posts. Consider opening a free e-mail account at Google, Yahoo!, MSN, or another service and using that exclusively for Google Groups.

# POST
## a new message

When you register for Google Groups and sign in, as discussed in task #76, you can post replies to existing newsgroup messages or post new messages to start your own discussions. Whenever you click a link that connects you to a specific newsgroup, Google Groups displays the Post a New Message to *Newsgroup* link, with the newsgroup's name in place of *Newsgroup*. You can click a newsgroup's link to open it and read a list of messages recently posted to it.

Just above the list of messages and to the right is the Post a New Message to *Newsgroup* link. You can click this link to display a page that enables you to compose and post a new message to the newsgroup. When posted, your message is not added to any existing discussion thread, but appears on its own, ready to start a new thread. Other users can then post a reply to your message or e-mail a reply directly to you.

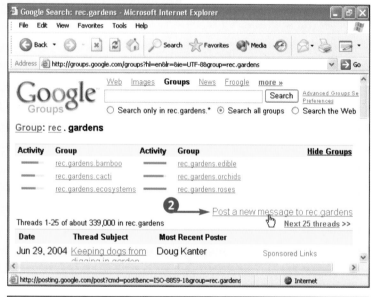

① Display a newsgroup in which you want to post a message.

*Note: Refer to tasks #71, #72, and #73 for information on how to find newsgroups.*

② Click Post a New Message to *Newsgroup*, with the newsgroup's name in place of *Newsgroup*.

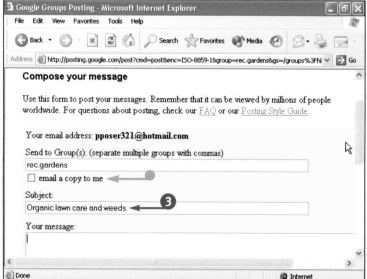

Google Groups displays the Compose Your Message page with a message addressed to the current newsgroup.

③ Type a brief description of the message.

● You can click here to e-mail yourself a copy of the message.

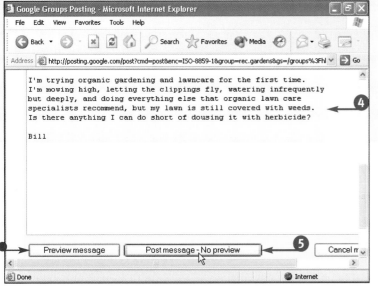

4 Type your message.

● You can click Preview Message to view the message before posting it.

5 Click Post Message – No Preview.

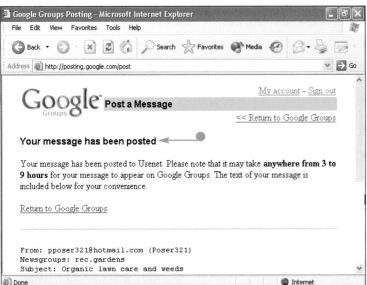

● Google Groups posts the message and displays a confirmation message like this.

---

## TIPS

### Did You Know?

To receive replies via e-mail, add your request to the message you post by clicking the Email a Copy to Me option (☐ changes to ☑). If you post a question that someone successfully answers in an e-mail message, return to the newsgroup and post a message to your original message, thanking anyone who has helped and including the answer to the question or the resolution to the problem you were having. This is considered proper etiquette in newsgroups.

### Did You Know?

Google immediately posts your message to the specified newsgroup, but your message may not appear in Google Groups for several hours. You can check your message later, as shown in task #78.

### Important!

If you want to post a test message to see how Google Groups works, post the message in the newsgroup alt.newbies. Posting test messages in topic-specific newsgroups is considered bad form.

# LOCATE A MESSAGE
## that you posted

When you post a message to a newsgroup through Google Groups, Google Groups posts the message within minutes, depending on the overall speed of the Internet and of the newsgroup server. Most often, the message appears on the newsgroup after a very brief delay. However, the message does not appear as quickly in Google Groups because of the way Google Groups operates. To make newsgroup messages fully searchable, Google must gather messages from the various newsgroups, process those messages to make them searchable, and then add the messages to its huge database of messages.

This process can take several hours, so do not expect your message to appear immediately in Google Groups in the newsgroup in which you posted it.

After several hours, however, you can search for your message using Google. The most effective way to search is by searching for messages posted from your e-mail address and for messages that include text that matches what you typed in the Subject box. By finding your message, you can determine whether Google Groups successfully posted it, and you can see if anyone has responded to it.

① Type **groups.google.com** and press Enter.

② Click Advanced Groups Search.

The Advanced Groups Search page appears.

③ Click here and type your e-mail address.

④ Click Google Search.

Google Groups displays links to all messages you posted from this address that it has indexed.

⑤ Click the link for the message that you want to read.

**DIFFICULTY LEVEL**

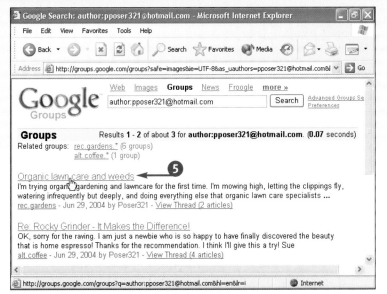

Your browser displays the contents of your message.

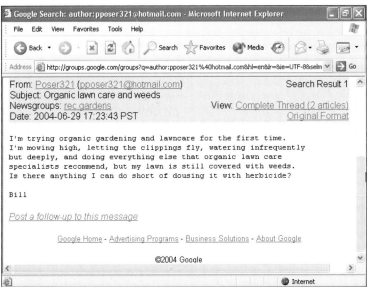

## Did You Know?

You cannot read the messages that appear in Google Groups by using a standard newsgroup reader, such as Outlook Express or Netscape Mail & Newsgroups. You can read them only using a Web browser. However, you can access newsgroups using a newsgroup reader. If you do so, you can use your newsgroup reader to determine if Google Groups successfully posted your message. You can usually access your posted messages much more quickly using a newsgroup reader than you can through Google Groups.

## Did You Know?

If you post a message and then decide that posting the message was not a good idea, you can remove the posted message. Google refers to this as *nuking* a post, which you can learn how to do in task #79.

## Did You Know?

You can prevent Google from archiving a message. To do so, type **X-No-archive: yes** in the first line of your message.

# NUKE
## a posted message

You may post a message and then later realize that you do not want the message posted. Perhaps you posted a question that someone had already answered in the same newsgroup, or you posted a snide reply that you later regret. Although you should read a newsgroup carefully before posting a message and should not knowingly post messages that may offend others, making an occasional mistake is common. Fortunately, Google Groups can help you recover from such errors by *nuking* a message — removing it from a newsgroup. Generally,

you cannot nuke a message that someone else posted, but you can nuke messages that you post.

Google features an automatic removal tool that enables you to remove Web pages, subdirectories, images, outdated links, posted newsgroup messages, and other items from its archive. You simply go to the page that contains the automatic removal tool and specify the item or items that you want to delete. You may need to reenter your logon information to confirm that you are who you claim to be. You can then choose to have any messages that you posted deleted.

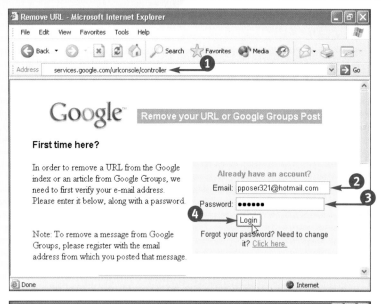

① Type **services.google.com/ urlconsole/controller** and press Enter.

② If prompted to enter your e-mail address and password, click here and type your e-mail address.

③ Click here and type your password.

④ Click Login.

The Automatic Removal Tool page appears.

⑤ Click the link for removing a posted newsgroup message.

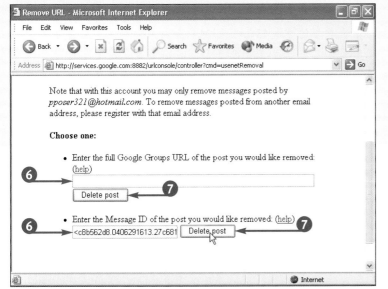

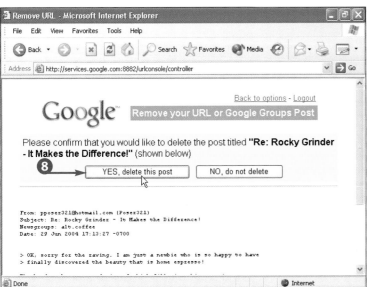

**6** Enter the full Google Groups URL or message ID of the message that you want to nuke.

**Note:** *You can obtain the URL by displaying the message and copying the URL from your browser's address bar.*

**Note:** *The message ID appears when you display a message and click the Original Format link.*

**7** Click Delete Post.

Google Groups displays a message, prompting you to confirm your request to delete your message.

**8** Click Yes, Delete This Post.

The automatic removal tool removes the specified newsgroup message, typically within 24 hours.

## Did You Know?

To remove a message you posted using an e-mail address that is no longer valid, contact Google support at groups-support@google.com. Include the following information in your message: your full name and contact information, including a valid e-mail address; the Google Groups URL or message ID for each message you want removed; a statement indicating that you swear under oath that you are the person who posted the message or are authorized to remove it; and your electronic signature.

## Did You Know?

You have very little recourse when it comes to deleting messages that you have not posted yourself. If someone posts a message that you feel is offensive or libelous, try to resolve the issue with the person directly. If you cannot resolve the issue, and the person is a Google Groups user, you can report the problem to Google, as discussed in the next task.

# REPORT NEWSGROUP ABUSE
## to Google

Google Groups users must agree to Google's terms of service in order to remain in good standing with Google and continue to use its service. If you notice that a Google Groups user is not adhering to the terms of service — perhaps by posting offensive messages, posting unsolicited advertisements, or spamming you — you can report the abuse to Google to have them investigate the activity. If Google determines that the user is, in fact, abusing newsgroup access, Google may warn the user or terminate the user's account. This may not stop the abuser because he or she can simply create a new account, but it may provide at least a temporary remedy.

To inform Google of possible newsgroup abuse, you can send an e-mail message describing the incident in question. Your message must include a complete header of the posted message.

Google intervenes only in extreme cases in which the abuse is blatant and widespread. If a Google user is being obnoxious or offensive, Google encourages people in the newsgroup to express their displeasure directly to the person.

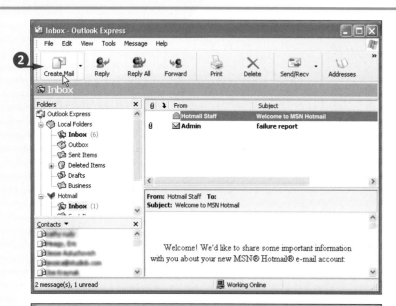

① Open your e-mail program.

② Click the button for creating a new message.

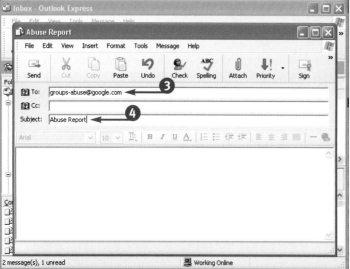

Your e-mail program opens a new message.

③ Click in the To: box and type **groups-abuse@google.com**.

④ Type a brief description of your message.

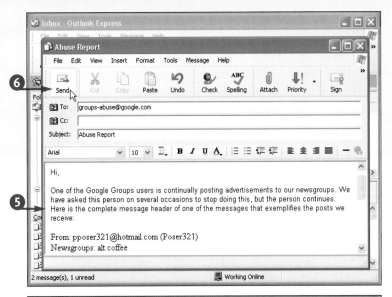

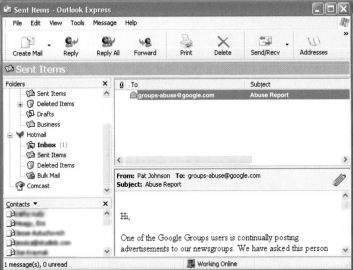

**5** Type your message, explaining the incident that prompted you to contact Google.

*Note: Be sure to include the complete message header of the offending message.*

**6** Click Send.

**DIFFICULTY LEVEL**

Your e-mail program sends the message to Google.

*Note: Google may not act on your complaint for several days, if it acts on it at all.*

**TIPS**

### Did You Know?

Google is not responsible for what its users choose to post in Usenet newsgroups, but it will respond to any incidents that break its terms of service agreement. Google does not police the Internet, however. If a user who is not a Google Groups member posts a message that is offensive of libelous, Google's options are limited.

### Did You Know?

To follow proper newsgroup etiquette, you should first read any newsgroup FAQs and several posted messages before replying to any messages or starting a new discussion. This helps you avoid posting questions that have already been answered and helps you tune in to the culture of the newsgroup. Also, follow these rules of etiquette: Post only messages that address the topic of the newsgroup; do not post the same message in multiple newsgroups; and do not advertise in newsgroups.

# Create and Maintain Your Blog

A *blog,* short for *Web log,* is a personal Web site that people often create to express their observations and opinions, maintain a journal of their experiences, or keep in touch with friends and family members. Unlike a Web page, which usually requires some knowledge of HTML, blogs require very little technical know-how. To update a blog, the *blogger* — the person who creates and maintains the blog — types a message and clicks a button to post it to the blog. Almost immediately, the blog software posts the entry, and it appears online, where visitors can view it in their Web browsers. Blogs typically display entries in the order in which the blogger posts them, presenting the most recent entry first. Blogs often encourage visitors to add their opinions and insights as comments.

This chapter provides a brief overview of blogging, showing you how to start your own blog using Google's Blogger. The chapter then offers techniques and tips to enhance your blog, link it to other sources of news and information, make it more interactive, and promote it so that more people can find it and contribute to it. With the tasks in this chapter, you can create and maintain a blog that draws visitors from all over the world and fosters a community in which you can share your life, your opinions, your art, and everything else you have to offer.

# Top 100

# Create your own
# BLOG

Many users avoid trying to establish a presence on the Web because the mere thought of creating a Web page and managing a site seems overwhelming. They think that they need to learn HTML or master a Web page editor in order to create a site that looks somewhat attractive. And after they create the site, they need to learn to use other software to transfer the Web page to a Web server. Of course, some Web hosts, such as Yahoo!, provide tools to simplify the process, but using those tools daily to keep the pages up-to-date can be more work than most users want to invest.

Several blog hosting services on the Web provide users with simplified tools for creating and maintaining a presence on the Web via a personal blog. In most cases, creating a blog consists of answering a few questions and completing an online form. This task shows you how to connect to Google's Blogger, one of the more popular blog hosting services, and use its tools to create your own custom blog.

❶ Type **www.blogger.com** and press Enter.

Blogger's home page appears.

❷ Click Create Your Blog Now.

Blogger prompts you to enter the information required to register for a new account.

❸ Type the requested information.

❹ Click here to accept Blogger's Terms of Service.

❺ Click Continue.

Blogger prompts you to name your blog.

6 Type a title for your blog.

7 Type an entry to complete the blog address.

8 Click Continue and follow the on-screen instructions to create your blog.

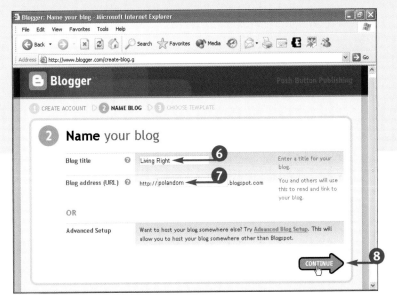

After Blogger creates your blog, it displays a screen where you can type your first entry.

9 Type your message here.

● You can click Preview to view your post before publishing it.

10 Click Publish Post.

Blogger publishes your entry on your blog, where visitors can view it.

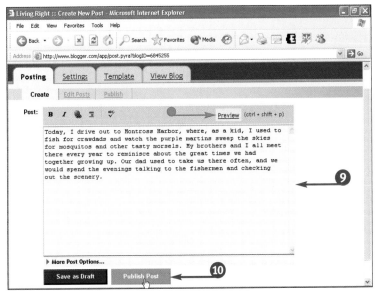

 **TIPS**

### Important!
When blogging, realize that most blogs are public. An unflattering description of a coworker or acquaintance that you post on a public blog may cause problems for you later. Even messages posted to a private blog can be made public, if one of the people with access to your blog chooses to make it public. Be discreet.

### More Options!
Several other companies offer free blog hosting, including Blog-City at www.blog-city.com, Blogit at www.blogit.com, LiveJournal.com at www.livejournal.com, eBloggy at www.ebloggy.com, and Xanga.com at www.xanga.com.

### Did You Know?
If you have a Web server where you would like to store your blog, you can download and install a program, such as Moveable Type, on the Web server that enables you to edit your blog right on your Web server. You can download a copy of Moveable Type from www.moveabletype.org.

# Blog a Web site or
# NEWS SOURCE

If you use your blog to present other sources of information on the Web or to comment on information and reports from other Web sites or blogs, you may want to link your blog to those sites. In many cases, you can simply copy a site's URL and paste it as a link into one of your posts. If you are using Blogger as your blog host, an easier way to add a link to another site is to use the BlogThis! button in the Google toolbar, introduced in task #34.

This task assumes that you have installed the Google toolbar and activated it in Internet Explorer. It also assumes that you use Blogger as your blog host. If you use Blogger and the Google toolbar is turned on in Internet Explorer, you can turn on the BlogThis! button and use it to add a link for any Web page or blog displayed in Internet Explorer to your blog.

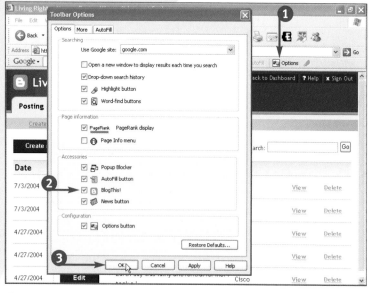

① In the Google toolbar, click the Options button.

The Options dialog box appears.

② Click BlogThis!.

③ Click OK.

The BlogThis! button (⬛) appears in the Google toolbar.

④ In your browser, display the page that you want to connect to your blog.

⑤ Click the BlogThis! button.

Blogger appears and displays the HTML source code for creating a link to the selected page.

⑥ Type any additional text before or after the HTML source code.

⑦ Click Publish.

Blogger publishes your comment, along with a link to the site.

● When you view your blog, it displays a link to the specified site.

## Did You Know?

You can add a link to a post without using the BlogThis! button (🔲). Highlight the address in your browser and press Ctrl+C. When typing your message to post, click the Insert Link button (🔳) to display the Insert Link dialog box and press Ctrl+V to insert the address. Click OK. Just before the `</a>` code, type the link's name as you want it to appear on your blog. For example, a link to Google's home page would look like this: `<a href="http://www.google.com/">Google</a>`.

## More Options!

To have the BlogThis! feature include text from a Web page or a blog to which you are linking, highlight the text before clicking the BlogThis! button. BlogThis! inserts the text as a quote.

# UPDATE
## your blog

Unlike a Web site that can continue to draw visitors for many months after the Webmaster stops updating it, blogs call for daily updates to keep visitors coming back. In many ways, blogs are more like news media than like personal Web sites. Visitors depend on the changing nature of your blog and on your fresh insights and observations to keep them engaged. In addition, if a visitor posts a comment to your blog and you do not respond in a timely manner, the person probably will not return any time soon.

Your blog's success depends on returning visitors and word of mouth, so if you want it to succeed, update it often — at least daily — and make sure that you include some interesting tidbits. Updating a blog is a fairly simple process, as shown in this task. In a matter of seconds, Blogger appends the message to your blog, where anyone can read it. One of the best features of blogs is that you can post your messages from any computer that is connected to the Internet.

① Type **www.blogger.com** and press Enter.

Blogger's home page appears.

② Type your username here.

③ Type your password here.

④ Click Sign In.

*Note: See task #81 to start a Blogger account.*

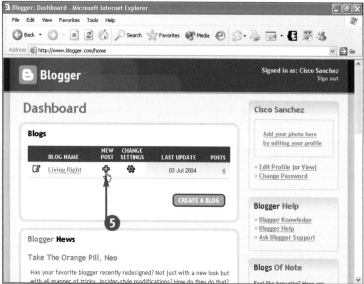

Blogger displays a list of your blogs.

⑤ Click the New Post icon for the blog that you want to update.

Blogger displays a blank text box for typing your message.

**6** Type the message that you want to post.

**7** Click Preview to preview your message before posting it.

**DIFFICULTY LEVEL**

Blogger displays your message as it will appear on your blog.

**8** Click Publish Post.

Your post appears on your blog.

### Important!
If you are going on vacation or are too busy to update your blog daily, publish a post indicating the date on which you will return. Otherwise, visitors may worry about you or assume that you no longer maintain your blog.

### More Options!
At the top of the screen you use to compose your posts are four tabs — Posting, Settings, Template, and View Blog. These tabs contain options for updating your blog, changing its title and description, modifying its template, and viewing your blog to check its appearance and content.

### More Options!
Before publishing a post, click Blogger's Spell Check button ( ) to check for any misspellings or typos.

# Make your blog interactive with a
# COMMENTS AREA

Interactive blogs — blogs that encourage visitors to post their own comments — are typically the most active blogs, as well. A comments area gives visitors a sense that they have a voice at your site, provides you with different perspectives, and can enrich your site with other observations and insights. To make your blog interactive, you can add comments capability. With comments, your posts appear as they normally do, but preceding or following each post is a Comments link that visitors can click to display a text box for typing their own observations and insights.

Early versions of Blogger offered no comments capability. If you wanted to enable others to post comments to your site, you needed to subscribe to a third-party comments hosting service, such as HaloScan. Now, Blogger has built-in comments capability. You can even have Blogger notify you by e-mail when someone posts a comment.

Blogger enables comments on all new blogs. You can choose to disable comments for each individual post.

① Log in to Blogger.

Blogger displays a list of your blogs.

② Next to the name of the blog for which you want to enable comments, click the Change Settings icon.

Blogger displays the Settings tab.

③ Click Comments.

Blogger displays the Comments settings for this blog.

④ Click Show.

⑤ Click here and select which users can post comments.

You can choose the default comment setting and choose to receive e-mail notices of posted comments.

⑥ Click Save Settings.

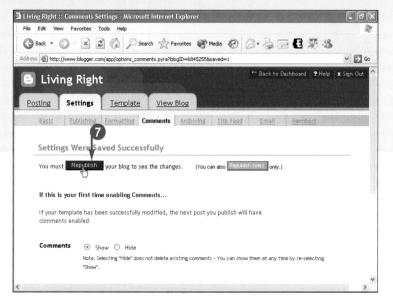

Blogger displays a message indicating that it has saved your settings.

**7** Click Republish.

Blogger republishes your blog to the server.

**DIFFICULTY LEVEL**

● When you post a new message, a Comments link appears, enabling users to post comments responding to your messages.

---

### Important!

If you choose to add a comments feature to your blog, make sure that you update your blog regularly and reply to any comments that call for replies. Otherwise, a user may feel ignored and choose not to revisit your blog.

### Remove It!

You can hide the comments that users have posted to your site. Display the Settings page, click the Comments link, and in the Comments section, click the Hide option (○ changes to ⊙ ). You can also disable comments for new messages that you post. Click the Default for Posts ⌄ and click New Posts Do Not Have Comments. Save your settings and republish your blog.

### More Options!

You can delete posted comments. Log in to Blogger and display the blog that contains the comment you want to delete. Click the link for the comment and then click the trash can icon (🗑) next to the comment.

# POST PHOTOS
## to your blog

Many blogs are primarily text-based, consisting of posted messages from the author and any comments that visitors choose to post. However, you can make your blog more pictorial in nature by adding one or more photos.

If you have photos that are stored on another Web server and you feel comfortable editing the HTML source code in your blog's template, you can use the HTML `<img>` tag to insert a photo. You place the cursor where you want the image inserted and then type the tag in the following syntax: `<img src="http://www.example.com/mypicture.jpg">`

replacing `www.example.com/mypicture.jpg` with the location and filename of the photo.

Blogger also enables you to post photos directly to your blog using the Hello BloggerBot, as shown in this task. BloggerBot is an add-on to Blogger that automatically resizes your JPG digital photos, adds any captions that you designate, and posts your photos to your Blogger blog. This saves you the trouble of having to find a Web hosting service to store your photos or add any complicated HTML tags to your page's template or your posts.

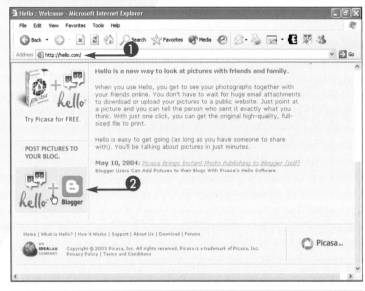

① Type **hello.com** and press Enter.

Your browser displays Hello's home page.

② Scroll down and click Hello + Blogger.

③ Follow the on-screen instructions to download BloggerBot, register, and install the program.

④ Open BloggerBot.

⑤ Click Send Pictures.

The Locate Pictures Using dialog box appears.

⑥ Click Use Explorer.

The Send Picture dialog box appears.

⑦ Navigate to the folder in which the photo is stored.

⑧ Click the photo.

⑨ Click Open.

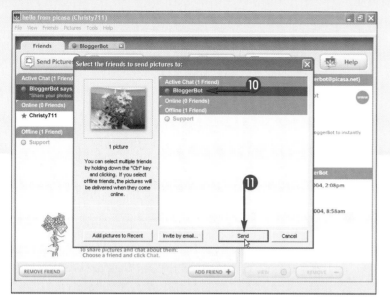

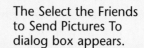

The Select the Friends to Send Pictures To dialog box appears.

⑩ Click BloggerBot.

⑪ Click Send.

BloggerBot adds the photo to the list of photos to send.

# 85

DIFFICULTY LEVEL

⑫ Type a caption for the photo.

⑬ Click Publish.

BloggerBot publishes the photo to your blog and then displays the updated blog in your Web browser.

## TIPS

### More Options!
The Hello program window includes a BloggerBot tab. Click this tab to view additional options for posting photos. You can select the size of the photos; choose the blog to which you want to post the photos, if you have more than one blog; select where you want the caption placed; and select a border preference.

### More Options!
Hello functions as a chat program, like America Online Instant Messenger, but specializes in exchanging photographs. You can click the Friends tab and click the Add Friends button to add people to your list of friends, if they are registered users of Hello, or invite them to join Hello, if they are not registered users.

# ATTRACT READERS
## to your blog

Your blog may turn up in a Google or Yahoo! search, but search engines and directories are not the avenues that most blogs travel to earn their fame. Bloggers use more of a word-of-mouth, grassroots marketing strategy that consists of letting friends, family members, colleagues, and various Internet communities know that they have a blog and that they want people to visit it.

To attract visitors to your blog, take one or more of the following approaches: Add a link to your blog to all your e-mail messages; tell all your friends, family

members, and colleagues about your blog; trade links with other bloggers — place links to their blogs on your blog in exchange for their linking their blogs to yours; and keep your blog up-to-date and interesting to encourage visitors to return and recommend your blog to their friends.

You should also create a profile on Blogger, as shown in this task, so that people can get to know more about you personally. This makes people feel more connected to you and your site.

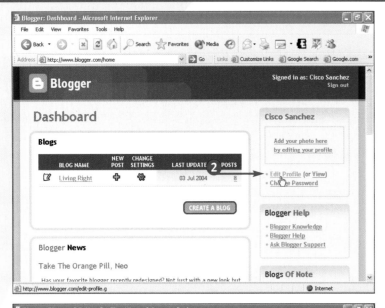

**①** Log in to Blogger.

Blogger displays a list of your blogs.

**②** Click Edit Profile.

The Edit User Profile page appears.

**③** Click Share My Profile so that other users can see your profile.

● You can choose whether to display your real name.

● You can choose whether to display your e-mail address.

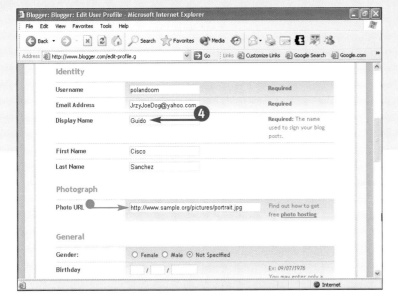

④ Scroll down the page and type a nickname in the Display Name box.

**Note:** *Blogger requires a display name.*

● If you have a photo of yourself stored on another Web server, you can enter its URL to display the photo.

**DIFFICULTY LEVEL**

⑤ Scroll down the page and enter any other additional information about yourself that others may find interesting.

⑥ Click Save Profile.

Blogger saves your profile.

---

## TIPS

### Did You Know?

During the writing of this book, Blogger was developing a tool to enable users to search Blogger profiles, but the feature was not yet available. The feature may be available by the time that you read this or sometime in the near future.

### More Options!

You can display information from your profile on your blog by adding special profile tags to your Blogger template. To learn more, log on to Blogger, click the Blogger Help link, click the Template Tags link, and click the Profile Tags link. All template tags are case-sensitive, so type them exactly as instructed.

### Did You Know?

You can share as much or as little information about yourself as you want to and edit the information at any time simply by repeating the steps shown in this task.

# List your blog with
# BLOG DIRECTORIES

Given that the Internet accommodates millions of active blogs, it's unlikely that visitors will stumble upon yours. Of course, automated search engines, such as Google, may add your blog to their search directories, but even so, if someone searches Google for a word or phrase that your blog contains, the list of returned sites may be in the millions, and your blog may end up on page 100 of the search results.

To more effectively publicize your blog, list it with various blog directories. Most blog directories

encourage blog creators to add their sites. Some of these directories contain only a few thousand blogs, increasing the chances that somebody looking for your blog will find it. This task shows you how to list your blog on Blogarama. The Web has several other blog directories, so when you are done at Blogarama, search for other blog directories and register your blog.

① Type **www.blogarama.com** and press Enter.

Internet Explorer opens Blogarama's home page.

② Click Add a Site.

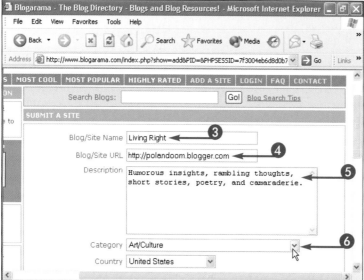

The Submit a Site form appears.

③ Type your blog's name.

④ Type your blog's address.

⑤ Type an accurate description of your blog, using as many descriptive words that you think a person may use to find it.

⑥ Click here and select the category in which you want Blogarama to list your blog.

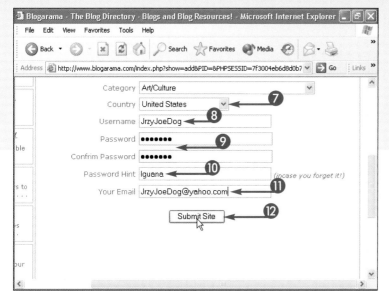

⑦ Click here and select the country in which you live.

⑧ Type a username to identify yourself.

⑨ Type a password in both of these boxes.

⑩ Type a password hint, if you want to.

⑪ Type your e-mail address.

⑫ Click Submit Site.

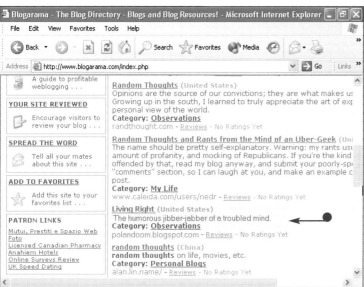

● After Blogarama verifies your site, which can take several days, and adds it to the directory, the site appears in the directory.

## TIPS

### Did You Know?

The username and password that you enter at Blogarama is for logging on to Blogarama; it is not the username and password that you use to log on to your blog-hosting service.

### More Options!

When you find other blogs that you like, consider contacting the blog's creator and asking if she is willing to link her blog to your blog. To add a link to someone else's blog, insert the following code in your blog template, replacing the italicized text with text that points to the correct destination:

```
<a href="http://www.site
name.com/">Site Title</a>.
```

### More Options!

Forums that address topics related to your blog can be a great place to advertise your blog. Make sure that you include a link to your blog in your posts to the forum, if this is acceptable practice in the forum.

# Check your blog's
# PAGE RANK

Google ranks pages according to their relative importance on the Web. Google keeps its criteria for determining a page's ranking secret, but one of the factors that contributes to determining a page's rank is the number of sites that link to the page.

If you recently created a blog, you cannot expect it to have a high ranking. However, if your blog is well established and several other blogs and Web sites link to it, your blog may achieve a relatively high page rank in a Google search. You can check your

page rank by installing the Google toolbar, as shown in task #34, and then opening your blog in your Web browser, as shown in this task.

If you search for your blog on Google and it does not appear in the search results, do not be discouraged. You can begin to increase the relative importance of your page by growing your audience and encouraging others to link to your site. See task #86 and task #87 for some ideas.

① Install the Google toolbar, if you have not installed it yet.

*Note: Refer to task #34.*

② If the Google toolbar is not visible, right-click any of your Web browser's toolbars.

③ Click Google.

The Google toolbar appears.

④ Type the address of your blog.

⑤ Click Go or press Enter.

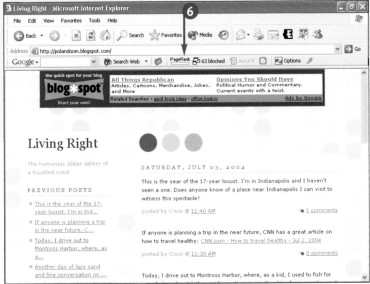

Your browser opens your blog.

**6** View the page rank.

**DIFFICULTY LEVEL**

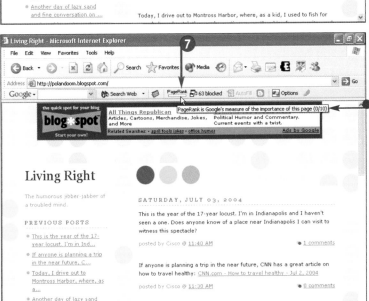

**7** Rest the mouse cursor on the page rank.

● A ToolTip appears, displaying the significance of the ranking and the numerical equivalent of what the page rank gauge displays.

The page in this example has a rank of 0/10, which means that it has no Google ranking yet.

**TIPS**

**Try This!**

You can submit the URL of your blog to Google to have it included in its search index. Go to www.google.com/addurl.html. Other search sites, such as Yahoo!, offer similar features.

**Try This!**

If your page has a fairly high page rank, open Google's search page at www.google.com and search for your page using various search phrases to describe it. This gives you some idea of how likely or unlikely it is that somebody may find your page using a search engine or index.

**Try This!**

Many users set up blogs intending to use them only for family and friends. To prevent search bots from adding your blog to a searchable index, display your blog's template page and type the following tag between the `<head>` and `</head>` tags near the top of the template: `<meta name="robots" content="noindex, nofollow" />`.

# EARN MONEY
## with Google AdSense

You can use your blog or any other Web site to earn money through Google's AdSense program, especially if you have a well-established site that draws a great deal of traffic.

Google AdSense enables you to have advertisements from Google sponsors appear on your pages. If a user clicks a link for one of the ads, you earn money. The ads are context-sensitive to fit in with the content of your site and make them appear unobtrusive.

You must apply for the AdSense program, and then Google must approve your application, typically

within two to three days. Google then supplies you the HTML source code that you can paste into your Blogger template to add Google ads to your blog. Within minutes after you paste in the code and publish your site to the Web, you can expect the ads to begin appearing.

Google AdSense examines any pages that include the AdSense source code, and based on the keywords it finds on your pages, it delivers advertisements targeted to the likely needs of your audience.

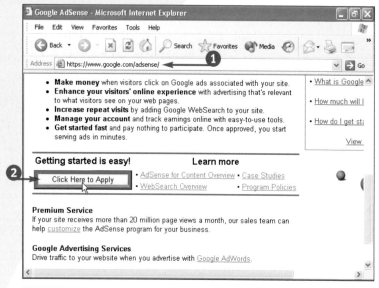

① Type **www.google.com/adsense** and press Enter.

The Google AdSense page appears.

② Scroll down the page and click Click Here to Apply.

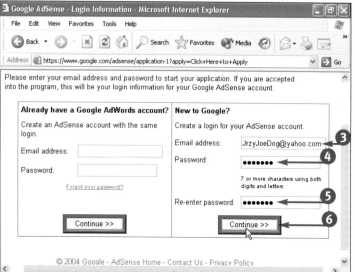

The Login Information page appears.

③ Click here and type your e-mail address.

④ Click here and type a password consisting of seven or more characters.

⑤ Click here and retype the password that you typed in step **4**.

⑥ Click Continue.

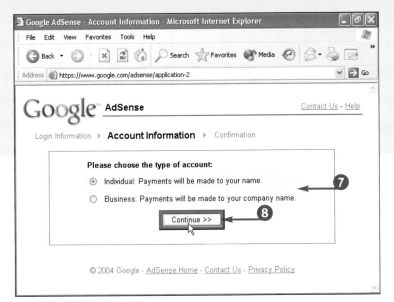

 **# 89**

Google prompts you to select an account type.

⑦ Click the account type that you want.

⑧ Click Continue and follow the on-screen instructions to complete the application.

**DIFFICULTY LEVEL**

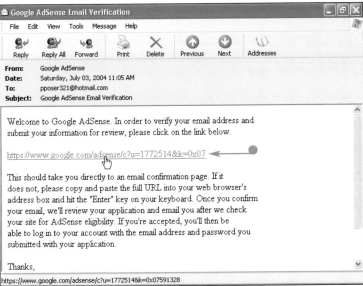

● Google e-mails you a message that contains a link you must click to verify your e-mail address.

Google then sends an e-mail notification in one to three days, informing you whether your application is accepted.

⑨ Follow Google's instructions to add the AdSense HTML source code to your Blogger template.

 **TIPS**

### Did You Know?

The source code that Google AdSense uses is a JavaScript that displays a banner across the top of your site. The banner has blue trim with a white background, but you can choose the color palette that you want, and Google automatically adjusts the JavaScript before you copy it. Google requires that you use the exact code it supplies. You are not allowed to edit the JavaScript to reduce the size of the banner, for example.

### Important!

Blogs are typically less commercial than standard Web sites, so users may not welcome the ads on your blog. Consider waiting until your blog is well established before adding Google ads.

### Try This!

For more information about implementing Google AdSense on your Web site or blog, go to www.google.com/adsense/faq-tech.

# POST AUDIO MESSAGES
## over the phone

Although blogs primarily publish text and images, you can add audio content to your blog. If you feel comfortable editing the source code in your blog's template and you have audio files stored on another Web server, you can add the `<object>` HTML tag to your blog to play background music or use the `<a>` tags to insert links to sound files.

An easier, and relatively new, way to add an audio component to your blog is to call your blog on the phone and leave a voice message. Blogger uses Audioblogger, a third-party product offered in

partnership with Blogger, to add phone message capability to your blog. With Audioblogger, you use your phone to dial the specified number, and then you speak your message into the phone. When you hang up, Audioblogger posts your message as a link that visitors can click to listen to the message.

Audioblogger provides a way to keep your blog up-to-date even when you are away from your computer. It can also provide your blog with another personal touch that many visitors find appealing.

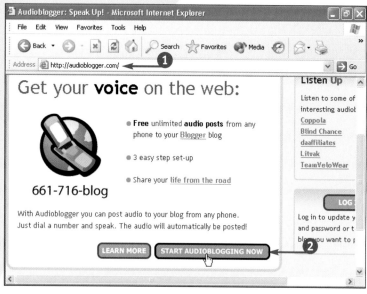

① Type **audioblogger.com** and press Enter.

Audioblogger's home page appears.

② Click Start Audioblogging Now.

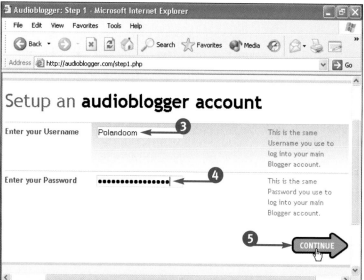

The Setup an Audioblogger Account page appears.

③ Type your Blogger username.

④ Type the password that you use to log in to Blogger.

⑤ Click Continue.

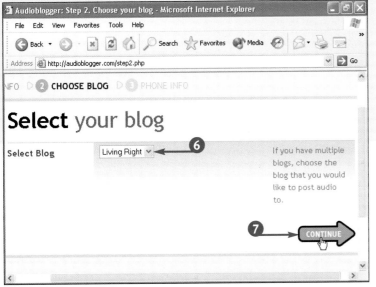

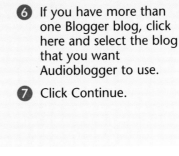

**6** If you have more than one Blogger blog, click here and select the blog that you want Audioblogger to use.

**7** Click Continue.

Audioblogger prompts you to enter the phone number that you want to use to make calls.

**8** Type the area code and phone number from which you will call.

**9** Type a four-digit PIN.

**10** Click Finish Setup.

Audioblogger creates an account, displays the phone number to call, and provides instructions.

## More Options!

Blogger also enables you to post messages via e-mail. To enable the e-mail feature, log in to Blogger and click the Change Settings icon (⚙) next to the blog that you want to be able to post to via e-mail. Click the Settings tab and then click the Email link. Enter the e-mail address from which you will post messages and fill in the Mail-to-Blogger Address box to specify the Blogger address that you want to use for accepting your posts.

## Did You Know?

During the writing of this book, Blogger offered Audioblogger as a free service, although most users incur long-distance charges when calling the number provided.

## Did You Know?

Audio posts are limited to five minutes. Each second of message time takes approximately 1 kilobyte of storage space, so a five-minute message is only 300 kilobytes in size.

# Explore the Power of Google Labs Tools

The developers at Google are never satisfied. They constantly search for innovative ways to improve and enrich Google for its many loyal and prospective users.

As Google developers experiment with new features and tools, they typically showcase these tools in a special area called Google Labs. You can visit Google Labs at any time to test-drive the latest offerings and provide valuable feedback to the Google developers.

This chapter introduces many of the Google Labs tools and features available during the writing of this book. This includes the Google Deskbar — a full-featured desktop utility that enables you to search the Web without launching your Web browser. This chapter also shows you how to perform personalized searches that match the search results to your interests, as determined from past searches you performed. Google Labs even provides tools for accessing Google with wireless Web–enabled cellular phones and PDAs.

Because Google Labs is a test ground for the latest and greatest features and tools in development, you can expect a few glitches. You can also expect some items to disappear from Google Labs — either to turn up as standard Google features or to be lost as failed experiments.

Whatever eventually happens to these Google prototypes, you can have a great deal of fun test driving them and exploring what the Google visionaries imagine for the future Google. As a tester, you also play an important role in Google's future development.

# Top 100

# Explore
# GOOGLE LABS

Google Labs is a testing ground. Experimental tools that you try out one day may be standard Google features the next. A tool that you enjoyed playing with last week may completely disappear if Google finds that it was unpopular, unworkable, or perhaps too popular for the service to support.

You can explore Google Labs regularly to learn about any new tools and features it is testing and to help provide feedback about whether you find a particular tool useful. You can even make a suggestion to improve a feature and help Google develop better services and products.

Whenever you visit Google Labs, it displays a list of any prototypes that are currently being developed and tested. It also provides a list of prototypes that have recently graduated from Google Labs to become permanent Google features.

Keep in mind that many of the prototypes covered in this chapter may no longer be available. Turn to this task often to check in with Google Labs, explore any new developments, and see which of your favorite prototypes eventually earn a permanent position with Google.

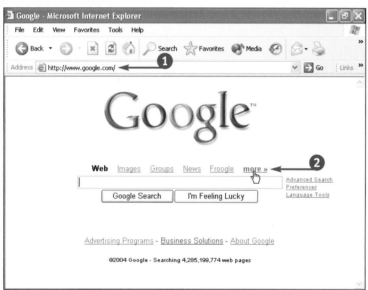

① Type **www.google.com** and press Enter.

Google's home page appears.

② Click More.

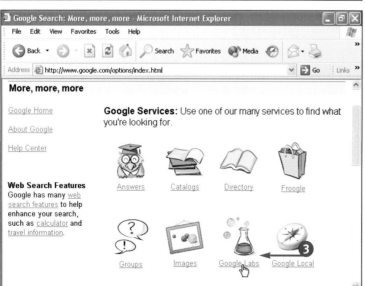

Google's More, More, More page appears.

③ Click Google Labs.

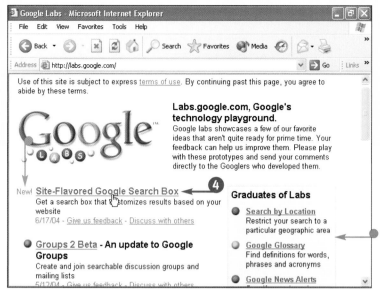

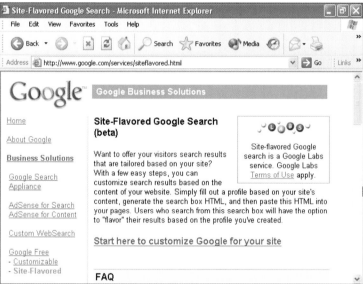

The Google Labs page appears.

● You can check the top of the list for new Google prototypes.

● You can check here for Google Labs graduates.

④ Click the link for a prototype.

**DIFFICULTY LEVEL**

Google Labs displays a brief description of the feature and instructions on how to use it.

## TIPS

### Try This!

After clicking the link for a prototype, examine the screen for additional links. The screen that introduces the feature commonly includes a FAQs link you can click to learn more about the feature and a Feedback link you can click to send feedback, via e-mail, to the Google engineer or researcher who developed the prototype.

### Did You Know?

Google is always looking to hire creative, gifted individuals. Scroll down to the bottom of the Google Labs page for a list of areas of interest. If you find a particular topic that interests you, you can click a link to send your résumé via e-mail.

### Try This!

Scroll down to the bottom of the Google Labs home page and click the Labs FAQ link for more information about Google Labs.

# Install the
# GOOGLE DESKBAR

You can install the Google Deskbar on your computer to add the power of Google to your computer's desktop. The Google Deskbar resides in the taskbar, typically located at the bottom of the screen. You can press any of several shortcut keys to call Google into action without running your Web browser — Ctrl+Alt+G to access a Google search, Ctrl+N for Google News, Ctrl+I to search for images, or Ctrl+F to search for products using Froogle.

The main feature of the Google Deskbar is the search box that resides in the taskbar. Whenever you want

to perform a search, you click the search box, type one or more words to describe an item or topic, and then click the search button. The Google Deskbar displays the search results in a small window that pops up out of the taskbar.

The search button that you click after entering a search phrase also functions as a menu for performing other types of searches, including movie reviews, thesaurus, and dictionary.

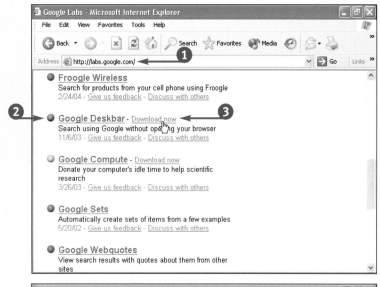

❶ Type **labs.google.com** and press Enter.

❷ Scroll down to the Google Deskbar.

❸ Click Download Now.

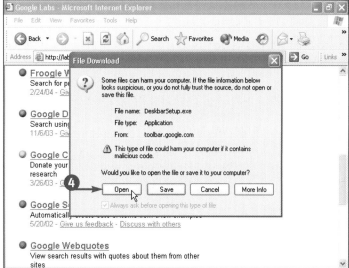

The File Download dialog box appears, enabling you to open or save the installation file.

❹ Click Open and follow the on-screen instructions to install the Google Desktop and display it in the taskbar.

⑤ Click the search box.

⑥ Type one or more words to describe the item or topic that you want.

⑦ Click the Search button.

Google displays the search results in a small inset window.

● You can click a link in the inset window to display its page.

## TIPS

### Did You Know?

The Google Deskbar offers several shortcut keystrokes that you can use to perform special searches, no matter which program you are currently using — Ctrl+Q for stock quotes, Ctrl+D for definitions, Ctrl+T for synonyms, Ctrl+F for products and services, Ctrl+N for headline news, Ctrl+U for Google Groups, Ctrl+I for images, Ctrl+L to perform an I'm Feeling Lucky search, and Ctrl+W to search the Web.

### Customize It!

The Google Deskbar is completely customizable. Click ▾ to the right of the search button (🔍) in the Deskbar and click Options. The Google Deskbar Options dialog box appears, which you can use to enter your preferences.

### Remove It!

You can remove the Google Deskbar at any time. Click ▾ to the right of the search button (🔍), click Help, and then click Uninstall.

# USE THE GOOGLE WIRELESS
## service on a portable device

If you have a wireless Web–enabled cellular phone or PDA — personal digital assistant, such as a Palm VII — you can access and use Google's powerful Web search capability from your wireless Web–enabled device.

Many sites offer wireless Web content that you can access, usually by subscribing to have specific content delivered to your phone. This enables mobile users to stay informed of the latest news, weather, and sports while they are away from their computers.

The wireless Web is also a great tool for obtaining directions, flight information, train and bus

schedules, movie and theater times, addresses and directions, and other specific information, no matter where you are.

What you can expect from the Google wireless service and how you set it up on your wireless system varies depending on the type of equipment and service you have.

This task introduces you to the Google wireless service and shows you how to access its help area on the Web, where you can obtain detailed instructions on how to set up the Google wireless service on your system.

① Type **www.google.com** and press Enter.

Google's home page appears.

② Click More.

Google displays links to additional features.

③ Scroll down the page and click Wireless.

The Google Wireless User Guide page appears.

④ Follow Google's instructions to set up the Google wireless service on your wireless device.

# 93

**DIFFICULTY LEVEL**

Image courtesy of Openwave Systems, Inc.

When the Google wireless service is set up on your device, you can access Google when you are away from your computer.

---

**TIPS**

### Did You Know?

Many wireless Web-enabled devices use Google as their default search engine. Before setting up the Google wireless service on your phone or PDA, check its menu system to determine if Google's wireless Web services are already installed.

### Try This!

If you have a handheld computer, such as a palmOne computer, you do not need to install any additional software or enter any special settings. Simply run your computer's browser and go to www.google.com/palm.

### Try This!

If you have a Palm VII organizer, you can download and install the Google PQA (Palm Query Application) on your computer and then use the organizer's HotSync tool to install the program. Installing the program places Google on the Palm.net menu.

# SHOP VIA PHONE
## with the Froogle wireless service

Even as Google's Froogle is just beginning to become a standard feature, Google is positioning it for wireless access as well. With the Froogle wireless service, you no longer need to be sitting in front of your desktop or notebook computer to find the best prices on merchandise. You can now shop while you are on the road. If you are out shopping and see something that you want, you can simply dial up the Froogle wireless service and search for the product to determine if you can purchase it from another merchant, perhaps online, for much less.

To use the Froogle wireless service, you need a cell phone, handheld computer, or PDA that has wireless Web-browsing capabilities. You can then enter the address for the Froogle wireless service to bring up a search box that prompts you to enter one or more words describing the product or service you want. On a wireless Web–enabled device, Froogle looks and functions much like it does on a standard computer system, although it appears in a much smaller window. Refer to Chapter 7 to learn more about using Froogle.

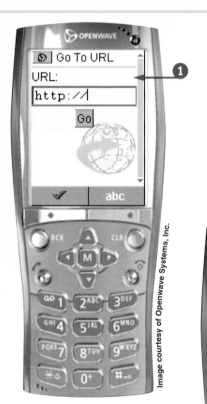

Image courtesy of Openwave Systems, Inc.

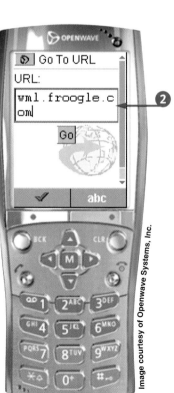

Image courtesy of Openwave Systems, Inc.

**①** Run the Web browser on your mobile device.

**②** Type **wml.froogle.com** and enter the command to open the page.

*Note: The method for typing and entering commands varies depending on the mobile device.*

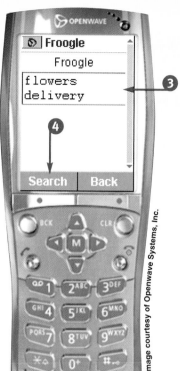

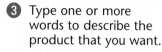

The Froogle wireless page appears.

**③** Type one or more words to describe the product that you want.

**④** Click Search.

# 94

**DIFFICULTY LEVEL**

● Froogle displays products or services that match your search description.

Image courtesy of Openwave Systems, Inc.

**TIPS**

## Try This!

Before you left on vacation or on a business trip, you may have forgotten about a birthday or other special occasion. Use Froogle to search for "gifts" or "flowers" and order a product online to have it delivered in time for the big day.

## Did You Know?

Even if you do not have a mobile device, you can download and install any of several mobile phone simulators to see how the wireless Web functions. The simulator used in this task is the Openwave Phone Simulator, which you can download from odn.openwave.com. Another fine simulator is the WinWAP browser, which you can download and use for a free trial period from www.winwap.org.

# MATCH YOUR INTERESTS

You can create a user profile describing your interests to have Google present you with search results that are more in line with your interests. From Google Labs, you go to the Google Personalized page, which is a search page very similar to Google's home page. One distinct component of this page is the Create Profile link, which leads to a page prompting you to enter information about your personal interests.

The page that appears when you choose to enter your personal interests does not request that you

enter any personal information, such as your name, address, or phone number. It only requests that you mark your categories of interest by clicking the check box next to various categories or subcategories.

After you mark your interests and save your preferences, Google places a cookie on your computer that identifies it, so when you return to Google, it can match its record of your interests to your computer. You can then perform a personalized search without having to specify your interests again.

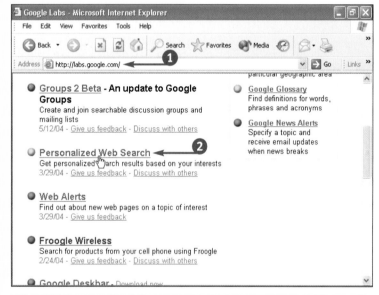

① Type **labs.google.com** and press Enter.

② Click Personalized Web Search.

Google's Personalized Web search page appears.

③ Click Create Profile.

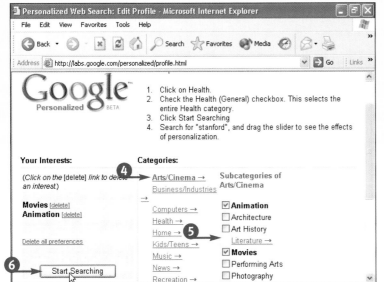

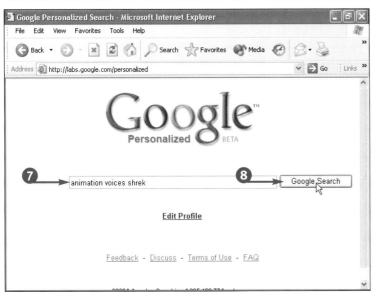

Google displays a list of links to commonly searched categories.

④ Click the link of a category in which you are interested.

Google displays one or more check box options for subcategories.

⑤ Click the check box of a subcategory in which you are interested.

You can repeat steps **4** and **5** to indicate additional interests.

⑥ Click Start Searching.

You are returned to the Google Personalized search page.

⑦ Type one or more words to describe the information that you want.

⑧ Click Google Search.

Google returns search results and displays a slider above the results that you can click and drag to indicate which results closely match your interests.

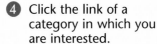

## Customize It!

When you click the Start Searching button to perform your search, Google places a cookie on your computer, so it can match your recorded interests to your computer the next time that you search. When your return to Google's Personalized Web search page, the Edit Profile link appears. You can click the Edit Profile link to change your interests.

## Remove It!

To remove the cookie that Google places on your computer, use your browser's options or preferences dialog box to access the cookie settings and then delete the cookie. In Internet Explorer, you can delete all cookies by clicking Tools, Internet Options, and then clicking the Delete Cookies button. In most cases, cookies do not store any sensitive information; they only provide a way for a Web site to identify your computer, but some users feel that they are an invasion of privacy.

# Receive notification of
# NEWLY DISCOVERED WEB SITES

Do you find yourself searching for the same topics every day? Then you can save time by having Google automatically perform your searches for you and notify you with an e-mail message of any newly discovered sites or pages.

Google provides this service, called Web alerts, for free. To use Web alerts, you open the Web Alerts page, type one or more words to describe the information you want, enter your e-mail address, and choose the frequency at which you want to be notified — once a day or once a week. At the

scheduled interval, Google sends you an e-mail message complete with search results of pages that contain the words you entered. You can then click links in the search results to launch your browser and display any pages that you want to view.

Google Web alerts help you keep abreast of the latest information without overwhelming you with outdated sites and information. This makes Web alerts especially useful for tracking a company's development, a celebrity's career, or links to your own Web site.

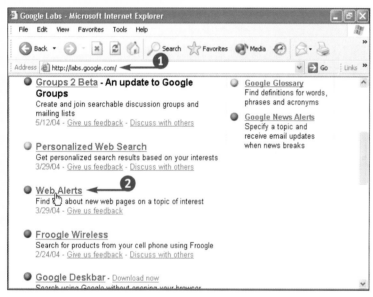

① Type **labs.google.com** and press Enter.

② Click Web Alerts.

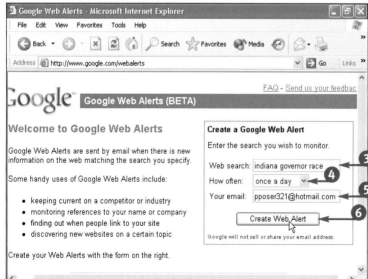

Google's Web Alerts page appears.

③ Type one or more words to describe the information that you want.

④ Click here and select how often you want to receive an alert.

⑤ Click here and type your e-mail address.

⑥ Click Create Web Alert.

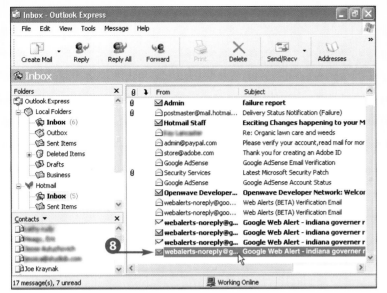

**⑦** Run your e-mail program.

If Google sent you a Web alert, it appears in your Inbox.

**⑧** Double-click the message description to open the Web alert in its own window.

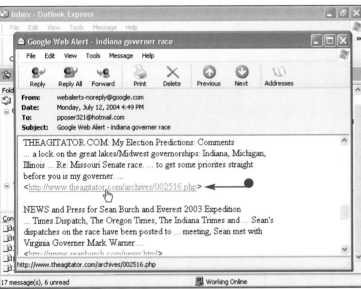

● The Web alert message contains links to any pages that contain new information that matches your search phrase.

## TIPS

### Important!

Before Web alerts become active, you must respond to a confirmation e-mail message that Google sends you. When you confirm your e-mail address, you let Google know that you are the person who requested the alert. This prevents people from sending Web alerts to other users who have not requested them.

### Did You Know?

Google does not share your e-mail address with other companies and does not sell it to spammers, so you can type your e-mail address with the knowledge that Google will use it only to send you Web alerts.

### Important!

Do not use Web alerts to have Google notify you of newsworthy information. Use news alerts instead to receive notification of updated news stories. To learn how to set up news alerts, see task #49.

# DONATE YOUR COMPUTER'S IDLE TIME

## to research

You can perform a public service by donating your computer's idle time to various research projects that Google approves. Google takes advantage of a technology known as *distributed computing* to place volunteer computers on a network of computers that work together to perform complex calculations and solve some of the daunting questions that researchers are trying to answer.

In most cases, sharing your computer does not negatively affect its performance. The Google Compute software that manages the sharing operation notes when your computer is idle and then uses it during these idle periods. When you begin using your computer again, Google Compute suspends operations, so it does not consume system resources.

For your computer to qualify as a volunteer, it must have the Google toolbar installed, as shown in task #34. It must also have a minimum of 64MB of memory and have Internet Explorer 5 or higher installed. If your computer meets or exceeds these requirements, it qualifies for the program. You can then download and install the Google Compute software on your computer to make it a part of this vast research network.

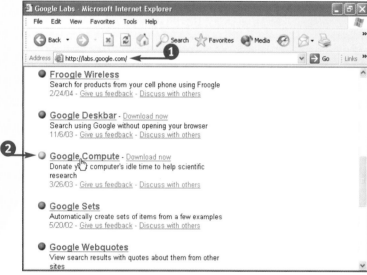

**①** Type **labs.google.com** and press Enter.

**②** Click Google Compute.

Google displays a page describing the program.

**③** Scroll to the bottom of the page and click Install Google Compute.

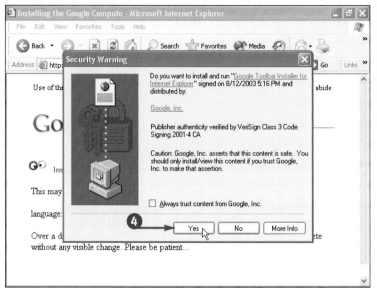

Internet Explorer displays the Security Warning dialog box, prompting you to confirm the installation.

④ Click Yes.

**# 97**

**DIFFICULTY LEVEL**

Google displays a screen thanking you for contributing your computer's idle time to the program.

● You can click ⊡ to the right of the Google Compute button — the button with the double-helix — to change your preferences.

### Remove It!
You can disable Google Compute at any time. Click the ⊡ to the right of the Google Compute button (🧬) and click Stop Computing. Google Compute immediately suspends any operation that it was performing.

### More Options!
An easier way to change settings is to click the Google Compute button and click Switch to Standard mode or Switch to Conservative mode.

### More Options!
Google Compute can use a great deal of your computer's system resources during idle time, which maximizes its contribution to research. You can limit the amount of resources used by entering your preferences on the Configuration page. Click the Google Compute button and then click Configuration Page. Google Compute displays the current settings. Enter your preferences and then click the Save Settings button.

# Generate search results with
# GOOGLE SETS

Google Labs has developed an interesting search tool called Google Sets that enables you to track down items that are similar to or related to other items in a list. For example, if you cannot think of a particular brand of automobile, you may enter **mercedes benz**, **rolls royce**, and **ferrari** to view a list of manufacturers including these three plus Porsche, Saab, Chrysler, and others.

How useful the tool is in helping find specific Web sites and information is open to debate, but using Google Sets is fun. You can enter the names of your favorite three movie actors to see how Google Sets completes your list. Or you can type three disparate search phrases, such as **john travolta**, **woody woodpecker**, and **small engine airplane** to see if these three items have anything remotely in common.

Google Sets is useful in helping extrapolate from a series of entries and help you remember a word or name. If you cannot think of the name of a particular diet, for example, you can enter the names of several diets you do remember, and then have Google Sets suggest the names of other diets.

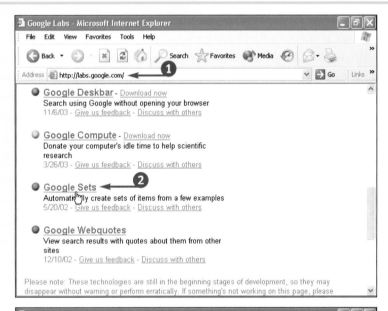

① Type **labs.google.com** and press Enter.

② Click Google Sets.

The Google Sets page appears, displaying several text boxes.

③ Type entries into two or more of the text boxes.

④ Click Large Set for a long list of results or Small Set for a shorter list.

Google Sets displays a list of results that are related to the two or more entries you entered.

● You can click the link for one of the results.

DIFFICULTY LEVEL

If you click a link for a Google Sets result, Google performs a standard search using that search phrase.

## TIPS

### Try This!

If you would like to share your opinion of or suggestions about Google Sets to Google, click the Feedback link at the top of the page. This runs your e-mail program and automatically addresses the message to the developers of the Google Sets feature. Type your comments or suggestions and click the Send button.

### Try This!

To discuss the Google Sets feature with other Google users, click the Discuss link near the top of the page. This connects you to a Google Groups discussion group where you can read messages posted by other Google users. To post a message, you must be registered to use Google Groups. For more information, see Chapter 8.

### More Options!

If you do not have any idea what to type in the Google Sets boxes, click a link for one of the examples at the bottom of the page.

# FIND QUOTES
## about a site with WebQuotes

A standard Google search displays links that point directly to pages that address a specific subject or topic. Google Labs provides a tool called WebQuotes that enables you to search for sites and view comments about the site from other Web sites. Using WebQuotes, you can obtain valuable insights and recommendations concerning a site before you choose to visit it. Think of it as a referral service for Web sites and pages.

You perform a WebQuotes search in much the same way that you perform a standard search. After typing the subject or topic of interest, you can choose the number of quotes or comments that you want Google to include with each item in the search results. By default, Google includes up to three comments or quotes. If no other site has a comment that pertains to a site in a list of results, Google still displays a link to the site with 0 comments. In place of the comments, Google displays a brief excerpt from the site.

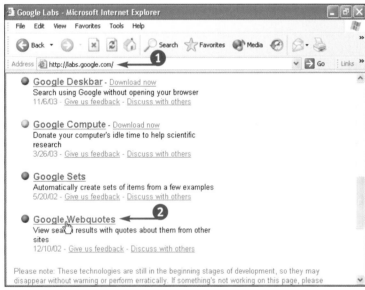

**①** Type **labs.google.com** and press Enter.

**②** Click Google WebQuotes.

Google displays the WebQuotes search page.

**③** Type one or more words that describe the topic of interest.

**④** Click here and type the maximum number of comments to include for each item in the search results.

**⑤** Click Google WebQuotes Search.

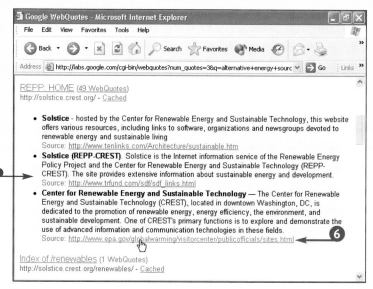

Google performs the search and displays links to any sites that contain all the words you entered.

● Any quotes appear here.

⑥ Click a link to one of the sources of the WebQuote.

DIFFICULTY LEVEL

Google displays the page that contains the quote.

## Try This!

If you have your own Web site, perform a WebQuotes search using a few unique words that describe its contents. If other Web pages contain comments about your Web site, Google's WebQuotes search displays the quote and a link to the Web page that contains the quote. This gives you some idea of what other people are saying about your site.

## More Options!

Each item in the list of search results includes a Cached link that you can click to view a copy of the page that Google has stored in its cache. Sometimes, comments refer to the cached version of the page rather than the newer version of the page that appears if you click the page's link.

# Create a
# SITE-FLAVORED GOOGLE SEARCH BOX

If you have a personal Web site and would like to provide visitors with a powerful search tool, you can add Google Free search or Google Free SafeSearch to your Web pages. You can go to www.google.com/services/websearch.html to learn about the various search services that Google offers. Large businesses can choose from several pay services, but individuals and small businesses can click the Google Free WebSearch link to access free Google search tools for their sites.

During the writing of this book, Google Labs was offering another free tool for searching the Web — the site-flavored Google search box. To create a custom site-flavored Google search box, you specify topic categories and subcategories that best describe the content on your site. Google then generates custom HTML source code that you can copy and paste into your Web document.

① Type **labs.google.com** and press Enter.

The Google Labs home page appears.

② Click Site-Flavored Google Search Box.

The Google Business Solutions page appears.

③ Click Start Here to Customize Google for Your Site.

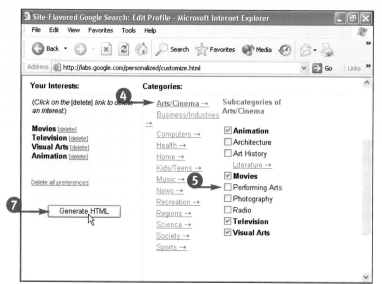

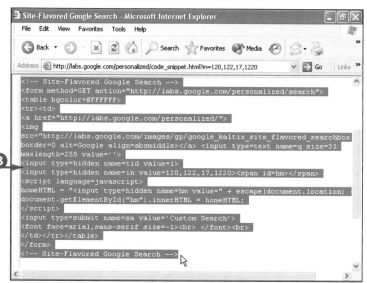

Google displays a list of available categories.

④ Click the link of a category that you want to add.

**100**

**DIFFICULTY LEVEL**

⑤ Click the check box for a subcategory that describes information included on your Web site.

⑥ Repeat steps **4** and **5** to mark additional categories.

⑦ Click Generate HTML.

Google generates the HTML source code required to display the site-flavored search box on your Web page.

⑧ Click and drag over the HTML source code to highlight it.

⑨ Press Ctrl+C to copy the highlighted source code.

⑩ Paste the source code into your HTML document, where you want the site-flavored search box to appear.

## TIPS

### Important!

HTML source code includes tags that mark the various elements that make up the page. The main portion of the HTML document is bracketed by `<body>` and `</body>` to mark the portion of the Web page that appears when a browser opens the page. Make sure that you paste the source code for the site-flavored search box somewhere between the two `<body>` tags.

### Did You Know?

The tag `<!– Site-Flavored Google Search –>` that appears at the beginning and end of the code for creating the site-flavored search box is a comment that does not appear on your page. It is included to help Web authors see where the code begins and ends.

# Index

## Symbols and Numbers

## A

## B

# Index

# Index

# Index

Similar Pages link, 12–13, 75
Singingfish search engine, 41
site: search operator, 9, 17
site-flavored Google search box, 212–213
size
    of files versus image dimensions, 29
    searching for images by, 28–29
slash (/) as division operator, 60
sorting
    Froogle items by price, 141
    Google Groups messages, 153, 159
    news stories by date, 94–95
source: search operator, 101
spaces after search operators, 17, 23, 51
spam, 161, 168–169
special searches, recognition by Google, 114
spelling feature, 46, 48–49, 177
Stock Quotes link, 58, 59
stocks and mutual funds, 16, 46, 58–59
stocks: search operator, 16, 46, 59
street addresses. *See also* local searches
    finding maps for, 46, 54–55
    math operations misidentified as, 61
synonym search operator (tilde [~]), 15, 33
system requirements for distributed computing, 206

taskbar, Google Deskbar on, 196–197
tax forms, IRS, 42
technology-specific searches, 10–11
templates for blogs, 177
three-letter codes for airports, 57
ticker symbols for stocks, 46, 58, 59
tilde (~) as synonym search operator, 15, 33
titles of sites, search operators for, 16, 17
Toolbar Options dialog box, 86–89
toolbars
    Google, 76–83, 86–89
    hiding in Internet Explorer, 77
    installing Google buttons on, 72–73
    preparing for Google buttons, 70–71
topic-specific searches, 10–11
Translate This Page link, 62–63
translating languages
    button names and, 105
    in e-mail messages, 65
    foreign news stories, 104–105
    Language Tools page, 64–65
    on-the-fly, 62–63
    returning page to original language, 63

uninstalling Google toolbar, 77
units of measure, converting, 61
university searches, 10–11
Unrecognized documents, 45
updating blogs, 176–177
Use Moderate Filtering option, 36–37
Use Strict Filtering option, 36–37

Usenet, 148. *See also* discussion forums; Google Groups
users, preferences and, 5

video clips, finding, 40–41
View in Alphabetical Order link, 21
View Original Web Page link, 63
View This Article Only link (Google Groups), 158
View Thread link (Google Groups), 157, 158
viruses, checking documents for, 45
voice messages, posting to blogs, 190–191

WAV files, finding, 38–39
weather, checking for airports, 57
Web Alerts service, 204–205
Web browser accessories. *See* browser accessories
Web Buttons for Google toolbar, 88
Web logs. *See* blogs
Web sites. *See also* blogs
    adding links to blogs, 174–175
    AdSense information, 189
    Blogarama blog directory, 184–185
    for free blog hosting, 173
    mobile phone simulators, 201
    Movable Type blog software, 173
    personal, finding, 13
    searching for content in, 8–9
    searching for images in, 30–31
    site-flavored Google search box, 212–213
WebQuotes search tool, 210–211
whitelist for pop-up windows, 81
Windows Media audio (WMA) files, finding, 38–39
WinWAP browser, 201
wireless services
    Froogle, 200–201
    mobile phone simulators for, 201
    setting up, 198–199
    User Guide, 199
WMA (Windows Media audio) files, finding, 38–39
Word (Microsoft) documents, finding, 44–45
Works (Microsoft) documents, finding, 44–45
Write (Microsoft) documents, finding, 44–45

Yahoo!, browser toolbars from, 73
Yahoo! Maps site, 54, 55

zip code. *See also* local searches
    finding businesses by, 125
    finding people by, 53
zooming maps, 115

# Want more simplified tips and tricks?
## Take a look at these
### All designed for visual learners—just like you!

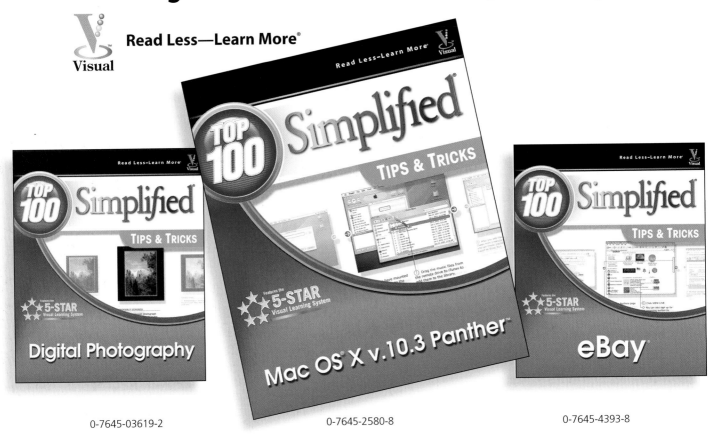

0-7645-03619-2    0-7645-2580-8    0-7645-4393-8

**For a complete listing of *Top 100 Simplified® Tips & Tricks* titles
and other Visual books, go to wiley.com/go/visualtech**

Wiley, the Wiley logo, the Visual logo, Read Less-Learn More, and Simplified are trademarks or registered trademarks of
John Wiley & Sons, Inc. and/or its affiliates. All other trademarks are the property of their respective owners.
Oct. 04

**Visual**
An Imprint of ⒲WILEY
Now you know.